TAX LIMITATION, INFLATION AND THE ROLE OF GOVERNMENT

By

MILTON FRIEDMAN

THE FISHER INSTITUTE • DALLAS, TEXAS

"The Future Of Capitalism"
was first presented as an address
to the Pepperdine University
Associates on February 9, 1977.
"The Limitations of Tax
Limitation" was previously
published by The Heritage
Foundation in *Policy Review.*
All other works were previously
published by The Institute of
Economic Affairs.

This edition has been published as part of the
publishing program of The Fisher Institute.

Cover design by The Richards Group

ISBN: 0-933028-00-8

Library of Congress Catalogue Number 78-73456

Printed in the United States of America

The Fisher Institute, 12810 Hillcrest Rd., Dallas, Texas 75230

FOREWORD

How better for the Fisher Institute to burst on the American intellectual scene than arm-in-arm with Milton Friedman? If there is a gentleman who exemplifies so well as Friedman the truths that the Institute means to propagate, why have we not heard of him?

A word about Friedman in a moment. A word about the Fisher Institute first. Every day there arise committees, foundations, interest groups, to study or grapple with the problems of the day. The Fisher Institute is such an enterprise. Then, again, there is much that sets it apart from the great mass of interest groups. Broadly speaking, the Institute means to change the world, but not through agitation — through ideas, rather.

The point is often lost on us that, in Richard Weaver's phrase, "ideas have consequences." So practical a man as former Treasury secretary William E. Simon affirms in "A Time for Truth" — probably the most-quoted book of the late '70s — that "ideas are weapons - indeed, the only weapons with which other ideas can be fought."

Ideas not only matter; they matter intensely. But how to get them across? For those whose idea is that economic freedom matters, the challenge is particularly stiff. The orthodoxy of the past 30 years or so would have it that economic freedom looks all very well on paper but that it had its day a century ago in the epoch of the robber barons. These are complex times, you see; and there must be leadership, direction, a firm guiding hand — which hand normally proves, in practice, to be a bureaucratic one. The orthodoxy, handed down from the towers of academe, has shaped the thinking of a whole generation of politicians and economists, not to say plain, ordinary intelligent people. Where freedom is not taught, who will think of it?

The solution, plainly, is to teach freedom. Yes, but how? How, in the face of the welfarist-collectivist consensus that sprawls heavily atop the community of thinking Americans?

"How" is a question that an invigorating organization named The Institute of Economic Affairs long ago answered in Great Britain, where, heaven knows, the consensus has pressed down far

I

more painfully than here. The IEA was the creation, in 1957, of Antony Fisher, an Old Etonian who piloted a plane in the Battle of Britain and survived to make a postwar fortune raising chickens. Fisher's endeavor brought together in London some of the country's most creative — because least wedded to socialist dogmas — intellects, who pointed out in lucid books and pamphlets the devastating consequences of welfarism and socialism run riot; who spoke plainly enough that their writings went out to professors and businessmen and opinion-makers the length of the kingdom; who analyzed with sufficient vigor and bite that they were taken more seriously with each passing year. Until, on their 20th anniversary in 1977, they were hailed by numerous commentators as the most influential economic group in all the land. To be sure, Britain's economic crisis remains unresolved, but it takes time for ideas to work their way thoroughly into the public consciousness. Even the watered-down Marxism of the Labor Party took decades to gain respectability.

So here is The Fisher Institute to attempt what the IEA has achieved in the way that the IEA has achieved it. The Institute is not "owned" by Fisher, though it bears his name by courtesy. It is, rather, a non-profit group whose founders include businessmen and academicians, all with a burning commitment to change the tenor of standard economic thought; to show the ordinary reader what freedom means, and how it works to help him and his family. There are organizations espousing free enterprise ideas all right — more of them probably than there have been in America's history. But I can think of none that is doing what The Fisher Institute means to do — namely, to hurl barrage after barrage not just at the smooth, smug philosophical facade of collectivism but at its consequences, which are dreary and dismaying. The Institute means to show what is wrong; and then it means to show how things can be made right again. Yes, again — for America's economic vexations — the swallowing up of public wealth by the taxman, relentless inflation, diminished incentive, a loss of confidence in the currency — were all but unknown to our grandfathers and great-grandfathers. They came about because a generation won over to ideas of government direction, if not of confiscation and redistribution, triumphed at the polls and

II

in the academy.

The Fisher Institute's appearance could hardly be more timely. The old collectivist notions shake on their pedestals, now that Americans have begun to realize that taxes are high and inflation is costly. It remains, perhaps, for the Institute to give the push that at last sends these notions crashing to the floor.

If so happy an opportunity exists, it is in no small measure due to Milton Friedman, who has lent his name to this, the Institute's maiden volume. Economists are not quite the "harmless drudges" that lexicographers, in Dr. Johnson's phrase, are — if only because ideas have consequences, bad as well as good. Too many economists are drudges all the same, speaking an arcane language at which the mind of the layman boggles. Not Friedman, whose gift for communication is hardly less impressive than those contributions to economic thought that in 1976 earned him the Nobel Prize.

Among economists, only John Kenneth Galbraith appears to share Friedman's facility with the spoken or written word, and Galbraith, as Friedman here assures us, is hideously wrong on point after point.

So are the collectivists wrong in general, Friedman assures us further in this collection of recent writings, including the 1976 Alfred Nobel Memorial Lecture.

They have sought to build us the New Jerusalem, or at least a pleasing suburb of that splendid city, where all live happily from government check to government check. Instead they have reared a slum that already is a candidate for urban renewal. Friedman is particularly struck by the example of Britain, which virtually invented free trade and free enterprise, only to surrender to confiscatory socialism a few generations later. The country's high inflation rate and stultifying tax policies are no surprise to him. He tells, even so, what to do about them, not just in general (try freedom) but in the specific (e.g., cut government spending from 60 per cent to 50 per cent of national income).

To be sure, Friedman is no blind ideologue. He knows the welfare state is the product of no dark conspiracy. "The great movement toward government," as he declares, "has not come about as a result of people with evil intentions trying to do evil.

The great growth of government has come about because of good people trying to do good. But the method by which they have tried to do good is flawed. They have tried to do good with other people's money."

And alas — so at least the collectivists would say — it hasn't worked. No, indeed, the founding fathers of The Fisher Institute nod in agreement: It hasn't worked. And here is their initial attempt to show us why. Do we now look for mass conversions to the faith of Adam Smith and Milton Friedman? I think not. As I have indicated, these things take time. But there is no time like the present for starting.

William Murchison
Dallas, Texas
October, 1978

William Murchison has been an editorial writer and columnist for The Dallas Morning News since 1973, and has contributed to a number of publications including *National Review*, *Human Events*, *Modern Age*, *The American Spectator* and *Conservative Digest*.

IV

TABLE OF CONTENTS

ABOUT THE AUTHOR

Milton Friedman was born in 1912 in New York City and graduated from Rutgers before taking his MA at the University of Chicago and his PhD at Columbia. From 1935-37 he worked for the U.S. National Resources Committee; from 1937-40 for the National Bureau of Economic Research; and from 1941-43 for the U.S. Treasury. From 1946 to 1977 he taught at the University of Chicago, where in 1962 he became the Paul Snowden Russell Distinguished Service Professor of Economics.

Dr. Friedman is now a Senior Research Fellow at the Hoover Institution of Stanford University. He has taught at universities throughout the world, from Cambridge to Tokyo. Since 1946 he has also been on the research staff of the National Bureau of Economic Research.

He is known to a wider audience as an advocate of a volunteer army (in place of the U.S. draft), a "negative" income tax (instead of partial or mass poverty programs), monetary policy and floating exchange rates. He is the acknowledged head of the "Chicago School" which specializes in the empirical — or experimental — testing of policy propositions derived from market analysis. Dr. Friedman was awarded the 1976 Nobel Prize in Economic Sciences.

A listing of Dr. Friedman's books, papers and public pronouncements in the field of economics is simply not possible in the limited amount of space available.

Chapter I
The Future of Capitalism*

When I speak of the future of capitalism I mean the future of competitive capitalism — a free enterprise capitalism. In a certain sense, every major society is capitalist. Russia has a great deal of capital but the capital is under the control of governmental officials who are supposedly acting as the agents of the state. That turns capitalism (state capitalism) into a wholly different system than a system under which capital is controlled by individuals in their private capacity as owners and operators of industry. What I want to speak about tonight is the future of private enterprise — of competitive capitalism.

The future of private enterprise capitalism is also the future of a free society. There is no possibility of having a politically free society unless the major part of its economic resources are operated under a capitalistic private enterprise system.

The Trend Toward Collectivism

The real question therefore is the future of human freedom. The question that I want to talk about is whether or not we are going to complete the movement that has been going on for the past forty or fifty years, away from a free society and toward a collectivist society. Are we going to continue down that path until we have followed Chile by losing our political freedom and coming under the thumb of an all-powerful government? Or are we going to be able to halt that trend, perhaps even reverse it, and establish a greater degree of freedom?

One thing is clear, we cannot continue along the lines that we have been moving. In 1928, less than fifty years ago, government at all levels — federal, state, and local — spent less than 10% of the national income. Two-thirds of that was at the state and local level. Federal spending amounted to less than 3% of the national income. Today, total government spending at all levels amounts to 40% of the national income, and two-thirds of that

*Reprint of February 9, 1977 address at Pepperdine University

is at the federal level. So federal government spending has moved in less than fifty years from 3% to over 25% — total government spending from 10% to 40%. Now, I guarantee you one thing. In the next fifty years government spending cannot move from 40% of the national income to 160%. (Legislatures have tried to legislate that the value of π shall be exactly three and a seventh but they cannot repeal the laws of arithmetic!)

We cannot continue on this path. The question is, will we keep trying to continue on this path until we have lost our freedom and turned our lives over to an all-powerful government in Washington, or will we stop?

In judging this possibility, it's worth talking a little bit about where we are and how we got here — about the present and the past. Let me say at the outset that with all the problems I am going to talk about, this still remains a predominantly free society. There is no great country in the world (there are some small enclaves, but no great country) that offers as much freedom to the individual as the United States does. But having said that we ought also to recognize how far we have gone away from the ideal of freedom and the extent to which our lives are restricted by governmental enactments.

In talking about freedom it is important at the outset to distinguish two different meanings on the economic level, of the concept of free enterprise, for there is no term which is more misused or misunderstood. The one meaning that is often attached to free enterprise is the meaning that enterprises shall be free to do what they want. That is not the meaning that has historically been attached to free enterprise. What we really mean by free enterprise is the freedom of individuals to set up enterprises. It is the freedom of an individual to engage in an activity so long as he uses only voluntary methods of getting other individuals to cooperate with him. If you want to see how far we have moved from the basic concept of free enterprise, you can consider how free anyone is to set up an enterprise. You are not free to establish a bank or to go into the taxicab business unless you can get a certificate of convenience and necessity from the local, state, or federal authorities. You cannot become a lawyer or a physician or a plumber or a mortician (and you can name many other cases) unless you can get a license from the government to engage in that activity. You cannot go into the business of delivering the mail or providing electricity or of providing telephone service unless you get a permit from the government to do so. You cannot raise funds on the capital market and get other people to lend you money unless you go through the S.E.C. and fill out the 400 pages of forms that they require. To take the latest restriction on freedom, you cannot any longer engage in voluntary deals with others or make bets with other people about the future prices of commodities unless you get the approval of the government.

Rising Taxation

Another example of the extent to which we have moved away from a free society is the 40% of our earnings, on the average, which is co-opted by the government. Each and every one of us works from the first of January to late in April or May, in order to pay governmental expenses, before we can start to work for our own expenses.

If you want to look at it still another way, the government owns 48% of every corporation in the United States. We talk about ourselves as a free enterprise society. Yet in terms of the fundamental question of who owns the means of production, in the corporate sector we are 48% socialistic because the corporate tax is 48%. What does it mean if I own 1% of a corporation? It means I am entitled to 1% of the profits and 1% of the losses. Well, the federal government shares 48% of your profits and 48% of your losses (if you have some previous profits to offset those losses against).

Once when I was in Yugoslavia some years ago I calculated that the difference in the degree of socialism in the United States and in Communist Yugoslavia was exactly 18 percentage points, because the U.S. Government took 48% of the profits of every corporation and the Yugoslav government took 66% of the profits of every corporation. And of course, those numbers grossly understate the role of the government because of its effect in regulating business in areas other than taxation.

Let me give you another example of the extent to which we have lost freedom. About a year or so ago, I had a debate in

Washington with that great saint of the United States consumer, Ralph Nader. I planted a question on him, because I knew what the answer would be and I wanted to extract the answer. The question I took up was the question of state laws requiring people who ride motorcycles to wear motorcycle helmets. Now I believe in many ways that law is the best litmus paper I know to distinguish true believers in individualism from people who do not believe in individualism, because this is the case in which the man riding the motorcycle is risking only his own life. He may be a fool to drive that motorcycle without a helmet. But part of freedom and liberty is the freedom to be a fool! So I expressed the view that the state laws which make it compulsory for people who are riding motorcycles to wear helmets were against individual freedom and against the principles of a free society. I asked Ralph Nader for his opinion and he gave the answer I expected. He said, "Well, that's all very well for a different society. But you must realize that today, if a motorcyclist driving down the road without a helmet splashes himself on the pavement, a government-subsidized ambulance will come to pick him up, they will take him to a government-subsidized hospital, he will be buried in a government-subsidized cemetery, and his wife and children will be supported by government-subsidized welfare. Therefore we can't let him!" What he was saying was that every single one of us bears on our back a stamp that says, "Property of the U.S. Government. Do not fold, bend, or mutilate."

That is essentially the fundamental principle that animates the Ralph Naders of our time — the people who want the power to be in government. You see it everywhere. You see it in a law which was passed a few years ago which requires the Treasury Department to report to the Congress a category called "Tax Expenditures." Tax Expenditures are taxes which are not collected from you because of various deductions permitted by the law (such as interest or excess depreciation). The principle is that you are, after all, the property of the U.S. Government. You work for the U.S. Government, and the U.S. Government lets you keep a little of what you earn in order to be sure that they'll keep you working hard for them. But the rest of it is the property of the U.S. Government. And if the U.S. Government allows you to deduct something from your taxes, it's providing for the expenditure. It's not a right that you have to keep it. It's theirs!

Other Freedoms Denied

We have gone very far indeed along the road to losing freedom. But you may say that I am talking only about economic matters, about whether you can enter a profession or an occupation. What about political freedom? What about the freedom of speech? How many businessmen have you heard in the past ten years who have been willing to stand up on some public rostrum and take issue with governmental policies? I have heard many a businessman get up and express general sentiments in favor of free enterprise and of competition. I have heard very few get up and criticize particular measures taken by government. And I don't blame them. They would be fools to do it! Because any businessman who has the nerve to do that has to look over one shoulder and see what the I.R.S. is going to do to his books the next day. And he has to look over the other shoulder to see whether the Justice Department is going to launch an anti-trust suit. And then he has to find two or three more shoulders to see what the F.T.C. is going to do. You can take any other three letters of the alphabet and you have to ask what they are going to do to you. In fact, a businessman today does not have effective freedom of speech.

But businessmen don't matter since they're only material business people. What about those people for whom we are really concerned — the intellectuals?

I asked my colleagues, suppose I take a professor from a medical school whose research and training is largely being financed by the National Institutes of Health. Do you suppose he wouldn't think three times before he gives a speech against socialized medicine? Suppose I take one of my colleagues in economics who has been supported by a grant from the National Science Foundation. I personally happen to think there is no justification for the National Science Foundation. (As it happens, I have never received a grant from them though I might have. It isn't that they have turned me down; I haven't asked them!) But nonetheless, do you suppose my colleagues would not be inhibited in speaking out? In fact, I have often said about the only people who have any real freedom of speech left are people who are in the fortunate position of myself — tenured professors at major private universities on the verge of retirement!

Freedom of The Press

Let me give you an even more chilling story about freedom of the press. The other day I got a clipping from an English paper from a friend of mine, indicating that the *London Times* had been prevented from publishing on one day because the unions, who have controlled the press, refused to publish it because the issue carried a story that was critical of the policies of unions. Do you mean to say that there aren't American newspapers which would hesitate very much before printing stories and articles that would be regarded as antagonistic by the trade unions on which they depend to produce their papers?

So there is no way of separating economic freedom from political freedom. If you don't have economic freedom, you don't have political freedom. The only way you can have the one is to have the other.

The Nineteenth Century

So much for the present, what about the past? The closest approach to free enterprise we have ever had in the United States was in the 19th Century. Yet you and your children will hear over and over again in their schools and in their classes the myth that that was a terrible period when the robber barons were grinding the poor miserable people under their heels. That's a myth constructed out of whole cloth. The plain fact is that never in human history has there been a period when the ordinary man improved his condition and benefited his life as much as he did during that period of the 19th Century when we had the closest approach to free enterprise that we have ever had. Most of us in this room, I venture to say, are beneficiaries of that period. I speak of myself. My parents came to this country in the 1890's. Like millions of others they came with empty hands. They were able to find a place in this country, to build a life for themselves and to provide a basis on which their children and their children's children could have a better life. There is no saga in history remotely comparable to the saga of the United States during that era, welcoming millions and millions of people from all over the world and enabling them to find a place for themselves and to improve their lives. And it was possible only because there was an essentially free society.

If the laws and regulations that today hamstring industry and commerce had been in effect in the 19th Century, our standard of living today would be below that of the 19th Century. It would have been impossible to have absorbed the millions of people who came to this country.

Why Regimentation?

What produced the shift? Why did we move from a situation in which we had an essentially free society to a situation of increasing regimentation by government? In my opinion, the fundamental cause of most government intervention is an unholy coalition between well-meaning people seeking to do good on the one hand, and special interests (meaning you and me) on the other, taking advantage of those activities for our own purposes.

The great movement toward government has not come about as a result of people with evil intentions trying to do evil. The great growth of government has come about because of good people trying to do good. But the method by which they have tried to do good has been basically flawed. They have tried to do good with other people's money. Doing good with other people's money has two basic flaws. In the first place, you never spend anybody else's money as carefully as you spend your own. So a large fraction of that money is inevitably wasted. In the second place, and equally important, you cannot do good with other people's money unless you first get the money away from them. So that force — sending a policeman to take the money from somebody's pocket — is fundamentally at the basis of the philosophy of the welfare state. That is why the attempt by good people to do good has led to disastrous results. It was this movement toward welfare statism that produced the phenomenon in Chile which ended the Allende regime. It is this tendency to try to do good with other people's money that has brought Great Britain — once the greatest nation of the earth, the nation which is the source of our traditions and our values and our beliefs in a free society — to the edge of catastrophe. It will be touch and go whether over the next five years Great Britain will be able to maintain a free society or relapse into collectivism.

When you start on the road to do good with other people's money, it is easy at first. You've got a lot of people to pay taxes and a small number of people with whom you are trying to do good. But the later stages become harder and harder. As the number of people on the receiving end grows, you end up in the position where you are taxing 50% of the people to help 50% of the people. Or, really, 100% of the people to distribute benefits to 100%! The *reductio ad absurdum* of this policy is a proposal to send out a rain of $50.00 checks to all and sundry in the next few months.

The Future

Where do we go from here? People may say, "You can't turn the clock back. How can you go back?" But the thing that always amuses me about that argument is that the people who make it and who accuse me or my colleagues of trying to turn the clock back to the 19th Century, are themselves busily at work trying to turn the clock back to the 17th Century.

Adam Smith, two hundred years ago, in 1776, wrote *The Wealth of Nations*. It was an attack on the government controls of his time — on mercantilism, on tariffs, on restrictions, on governmental monopoly. But those are exactly the results which the present-day reformers are seeking to achieve.

In any event, that's a foolish question. The real question is not whether you are turning the clock back or forward, but whether you are doing the right thing? Do you mean to say you should never learn from your mistakes?

Some people argue that technological changes require big government and you can no longer talk in the terms of the 19th Century when the government only absorbed 3% of the national income. You have to have big government because of these technological changes. That's nonsense from beginning to end. Some technological changes no doubt require the government to engage in activities different from those in which it engaged before. But other technological changes *reduce* the need for government. The improvements in communication and transportation have greatly reduced the possibility of local monopoly which requires government intervention to protect the consumers. Moreover, if you look at the record, the great growth of government has not been in the areas dictated by technological change. The great growth of government has been to take money from some people and to give it to others. The only way technology has entered into that is by providing the computers which make it possible to do so.

Other people will say how can you talk about stopping this trend? What about big business? Is it really any different whether automobiles are made by General Motors, which is an enormous bureaucratic enterprise employing thousands of people, or whether they are made by an agency of the United States Government, which is another bureaucratic enterprise?

The answer to that is very simple. It does make all the difference in the world, because there is a fundamental difference between the two. There is no way in which General Motors can get a dollar from you unless you agree to give it to them. That's a voluntary exchange. They can only get money from you by providing you with something you value more than the money you give them. If they try to force something on you that you don't want, ask Mr. Henry Ford what happened when they tried to introduce the Edsel. On the other hand the government can get money from you without your consent. They can send policemen to take it out of your pocket. General Motors doesn't have that power. And that is all the difference in the world. It is the difference between a society in which exchange is voluntary and a society in which exchange is not voluntary. It's the reason why the government, when it is in the saddle, produces poor quality at high cost, while industry, when it's in the saddle, produces quality at low cost. The one has to satisfy its customers and the other does not.

Two Possible Scenarios

Where shall we go from here? There are two possible scenarios. The one (and I very much fear it's the more likely) is that we will continue in the direction in which we have been going, with gradual increases in the scope of government and government control. If we do continue in that direction, two results are inevitable. One result is financial crisis and the other is a loss of freedom.

The example of England is a frightening example to contemplate. England has been moving in this direction. We're about twenty years behind England in this motion. But England was moving in this direction earlier than we were moving and has moved much farther. The effects are patent and clear. But at least when England moved in this direction and thus lost its power politically and internationally, the United States was there to take over the defense of the free world. But I ask you, when the United States follows that direction, who is going to take over from us? That's one scenario, and I very much fear it's the more likely one.

The other scenario is that we will, in fact, halt this trend — that we will call a halt to the apparently increasing growth of government, set a limit and hold it back.

There are many favorable signs from this point of view. I may say that the greatest reason for hope, in my opinion, is the inefficiency of government. Many people complain about government waste. I welcome it. I welcome it for two reasons. In the first place, efficiency is not a desirable thing if somebody is doing a bad thing. A great teacher of mine, a mathematical economist, once wrote an article on the teaching of statistics. He said, "Pedagogical ability is a vice rather than a virtue if it is devoted to teaching error." That's a fundamental principle. Government is doing things that we don't want it to do, so the more money it wastes the better.

In the second place, waste brings home to the public at large the fact that government is not an efficient and effective instrument for achieving its objectives. One of the great causes for hope is a growing disillusionment around the country with the idea that government is the all-wise, all-powerful big brother who can solve every problem that comes along, that if only you throw enough money at a problem it will be resolved.

Several years ago John Kenneth Galbraith wrote an article in which he said that New York City had no problem that could not be solved by an increase in government spending in New York.

Well, since that time, the budget in the city of New York has more than doubled and so have the problems of New York. The one is cause and the other effect. The government has spent more but that meant that the people have less to spend. Since the government spends money less efficiently than individuals spend their own money, as government spending as gone up the problems have gotten worse. My main point is that this inefficiency, this waste, brings home to the public at large the undesirability of governmental intervention. I believe that a major source of hope is in the wide-spread rise in the tide of feeling that government is not the appropriate way to solve our problems.

There are also many unfavorable signs. It's far easier to enact laws than to repeal them. Every special interest including you and me, has great resistance to giving up its special privileges. I remember when Gerald Ford became President and he called a summit conference to do something about the problems of inflation. I sat at that summit conference and heard representatives of one group after another go to the podium — a representative of business, a representative of the farmers, a representative of labor, you name the group — they all went to the podium and they all said the same thing. They said, "Of course, we recognize that in order to stop inflation, we must cut down government spending. And I tell you the way to cut down government spending is to spend more on me." That was the universal refrain.

Many people say that one of the causes for hope is the rising recognition by the business community that business enterprise is a threat to the free enterprise system. I wish I could believe that, but I do not. You must recognize the facts. Business corporations in general are not a defense of free enterprise. On the contrary, they are one of the chief sources of danger.

The two greatest enemies of free enterprise in the United States, in my opinion, have been on the one hand, my fellow intellectuals, and on the other hand, the business corporations of this country. They are enemies for opposite reasons. Every one of my fellow intellectuals believes in freedom for himself. He wants free speech. He wants free research. I ask him, "Isn't this a terrible waste that a dozen people are studying the same problem? Oughtn't we to have a central planning committee to decide what research projects various individuals are to undertake?" He'll look at me as if I'm crazy, and he'll say, "What do you mean? Don't you understand about the value of academic freedom and freedom of research and duplication?" But when it comes to business he says, "Oh, that's wasteful competition. That's duplication over there! We must have a central planning board to make those things intelligent, sensible!"

So every intellectual is in favor of freedom for himself and against freedom for anybody else. The businessman and the business enterprises are very different. Every businessman and every business enterprise is in favor of freedom for everybody else, but when it comes to himself, that's a different question. We have to have that tariff to protect us against competition from abroad. We have to have that special provision in the tax code. We have to have that subsidy. Businessmen are in favor of freedom for everybody else but not for themselves.

There are many notable exceptions. There are many business leaders who have been extremely farsighted in their understanding of the problem and will come to the defense of a free enterprise system. But for the business community in general, the tendency is to take out advertisements, such as U.S. Steel Company taking out full-page ads to advertise the virtues of free enterprise, but then to plead before Congress for an import quota on steel from Japan. The only result of that is for everybody who is fair-minded to say, "What a bunch of hypocrites!" And they're right.

Now don't misunderstand me, I don't blame business enterprise. I don't blame U.S. Steel for seeking to get those special privileges. The managers of U.S. Steel have an obligation to their stockholders, and they would be false to that obligation if they did not try to take advantage of the opportunities to get assistance. I don't blame them. I blame the rest of us for letting them get away with it. We must recognize what the real problem is and recognize that that is not a source of strength.

Faith In The Future

Where are we going to end up? I do not know. I think that depends upon a great many things.

I am reminded of a story which will illustrate what we may

need. It has to do with a young and attractive nun who was driving a car down a super highway and ran out of gas. She remembered that a mile back there had been a gas station. She got out of her car, hiked up her habit, and walked back to the gas station. When she got to the station, she found that there was only one young man in attendance there. He said he'd love to help her but he couldn't leave the gas station because he was the only one there. He said he would try to find a container in which he could give her some gas. He hunted around the gas station and couldn't find a decent container. The only thing he could find was a little baby's potty that had been left there. So he filled the baby potty with gasoline and he gave it to the nun. She took the baby potty and walked the mile down the road to her car. She got to her car and opened the gas tank and started to pour it in. Just at that moment, a great big Cadillac came barreling down the road at eighty miles an hour. The driver was looking out and couldn't believe what he was seeing. So he jammed on his brakes, stopped, backed up, opened the window and looked out and said, "Sister, I only wish I had such faith!"

Chapter 2
The Limitations of Tax Limitation*

Two down, 48 to go.

The approval on June 6, 1978, by the people of our largest state of Proposition 13 — a tax limitation amendment to the California Constitution — has given great impetus to the grassroots movement that Governor Ronald Reagan began in that state five years ago when he sponsored Proposition 1.[1]

The first victory for those who believe that government does not have an open-ended claim on the incomes of Americans came in Tennessee three months ago (March 7, 1978) when the people of that state, by a two-to-one majority, approved an amendment to limit the "rate of growth" of state spending to the "estimated rate of growth of the state's economy."

Similar amendments will be on the ballot in a number of other states this fall, and the prospects now look very good for their adoption.

The Jarvis-Gann Amendment, Proposition 13, will limit property taxes in California to one percent of assessed valuation. It will restrict increases in assessed valuation to a maximum of 2 percent a year except when property changes hands. In addition, it will require a two-thirds vote of the legislature to raise other taxes. It is estimated that this amendment will cut property taxes by more than half — or by some $7 billion.

Jarvis-Gann, it must be said, has many defects. It is loosely drawn. It cuts only the property tax, which is by no means the worst tax. It does nothing to halt the unlegislated rise in taxes produced by inflation. Proposition 1 was a far better measure and a revised version will be needed even though Jarvis-Gann has passed. Yet I strongly supported Jarvis-Gann. It does not cut taxes. It does raise obstacles to further increases in government

*Reprinted from **Policy Review,** Summer 1978

1. That proposal was preferable to the one adopted on June 6. It would have limited spending by the state government to a specified and slowly declining fraction of the personal income of the people of California. That amendment was narrowly defeated, as were similar amendments in two other states in recent years.

spending. Those in favor of more government spending mounted an expensive fear campaign financed in large part by big business (which apparently allowed its own fear of the politicians in Sacramento to trigger its unerring instinct for self-destruction). In this media blitz, the state employees' union leaders (naturally the core of the opposition) predicted that state services would be drastically cut, that thousands of policemen and firemen would be dismissed, and so forth and so on.[1]

In fact Jarvis-Gann will not have the dire effects its opponents threatened. The California givernment has a surplus of some $3 billion to offset the $7 billion revenue reduction. The remaining $4 billion is roughly 10 percent of the state and local spending now projected for the next fiscal year. Is there a taxpayer in California (even if he is a government employee) who can maintain with a straight face that there is not 10 percent fat that can be cut from government spending without reducing essential services? Of course, the reallocation of revenues to finance the most essential services will not be an easy or pleasant task, but that, after all, is just what we pay our elected representatives for.[2]

Tax Limitation Laws Are Not "Undemocratic"

Which brings us to an important point of political philosophy. It is my view that it is desirable for the people to limit their government's budget, to decide how much in total they are willing to pay for their government. Having done this, it is desirable for them to delegate to their elected representatives the difficult task of dividing that budget among competing good proposals. The

1. In their column for *The Washington Post* on June 1, 1978, Rowland Evans and Robert Novak reported from Los Angeles that some politicians were claiming that the referendum was "a fight between the haves and the have-nots." Evans and Novak concluded that this view was "almost surely wrong." They explained that "On the contrary, the establishment — business, labor, the big newspapers, the academic community, civic groups and practically every important elected official — vigorously opposes the Jarvis amendment."

They went on to point out that "in contrast, the amendment's hardcore support comes from lower income homeowners who are going under because of oppressive taxes. Their ranks, oddly, are swelled by substantial numbers of school teachers and other government workers who are first and foremost taxpayers . . . State Senator Bill Greene, a black Los Angeles legislator, told us he is astounded how many of his constituents are voting for the measure."

2. It is not without interest that California has the highest paid state legislators in the nation.

opponents of tax limitation laws charge that we are being un-democratic in proposing to tie the hands of government. After all, they say, don't we elect our state representatives and our congressional representatives in Washington to handle the affairs of government? I believe that if we are going to be effective in passing tax limitation laws, we must understand and make other people understand that these referenda are far from being undemocratic. I believe that the real situation is precisely the opposite.

The problem we face is that there is a fundamental defect in our political and constitutional structure. The fundamental defect is that we have no means whereby the public at large ever gets to vote on the total budget of the government.

Our system is one in which each particular spending measure is treated separately. For any single spending measure, therefore, there is always a small group that has a very strong interest in that measure. All of us are parts of such small groups. We are not talking about somebody else. As Pogo used to say, "We have met the enemy and they are us."

The vested interests are not some big bad people sitting on money bags; the vested interests are you and me. Each of us is strongly in favor of small measures that will benefit us and each of us is not too strongly opposed to any one small measure that will benefit someone else. We are not going to vote anybody out of office because he imposes a $3 a year burden on us. Consequently, when each measure is considered separately, there is considerable pressure to pass it. The proposers have greater force than the opponents (who are often called "negative" or "obstructionists") and the total cost is never added up.

The purpose of tax limitation is to remedy that defect. It will enable us to say to the legislature, "We assign you a budget. Now it's your job to spend that in the most effective way." The effect of removing this defect is to enable special interests to work for the general interest instead of against it. This is because with a given total budget, a special group that wants a special measure has to point out the other budget items that can and should be reduced. Each item that people want is a good item. There is no pressure on Congress or on the legislature, or very little, to enact bad legislation. The problem is that there is an infinite number of good and desirable proposals and you have to have some device to limit the appetite and that's the function of tax limitation.

The next time somebody says that tax limitation is undemocratic, we should ask him whether that means he is against the First Amendment of the Constitution. Because, after all, the First Amendment of the Constitition limits very clearly what Congress can do. The First Amendment says Congress shall make no laws interfering with the freedom of speech or the free exercise of religion. Consider what would happen if we didn't have that amendment. For any single measure restricting freedom of speech you might very well obtain a majority. I am sure there would be a majority to prevent the Nazis from speaking on the street corner. There might be a majority to prevent the Seventh Day Adventists or vegetarians from speaking — or any other little group you could name. But our Founding Fathers had the wisdom to roll it up into one and say we are not going to let each individual issue be decided separately by a majority vote. They said that we are going to adopt the general principle that it is not the federal government's business to restrict freedom of speech.[1] In the same way, what is being proposed today is the enactment of a principle that a government shall have a budget determined by the voters and that it will have to stay within that budget.

Government Spending Is the Real Problem

Right now total government spending — state, federal and local — amounts to 40 percent of the national income. That means that out of every dollar anybody makes or gets, forty cents is being spend for him by the bureaucrats whom he has, through his voting behavior, put into office. There is upward pressure on that percentage. The screws will be put on. The real problem for the future is to stop that growth in government spending. Those who are really concerned, who really are fiscal conservatives, should forget about the deficit and pay all their attention to total government spending. As we have seen, California and Tennessee have recently led the way toward the goal of a limit on government spending.

On the federal level, there have been moves to try to get

1. It was left to the states to deal with such problems as an immediate danger of violence, and so on.

a federal constitutional amendment providing for a balanced budget. I think, however, that is a serious mistake. It spends the energies of the right people in the wrong direction. Almost all states have a balanced budget provision, but that hasn't kept spending and taxes from going up. What we need on the federal level, as we need it on the state and local level, is not a budget-balancing amendment, but an amendment *to limit government spending as a fraction of income.* Recently a task force of the Southern Governors' Conference, which was headed by Governor James Edwards of South Carolina, has worked extensively to produce a government spending limitation amendment for the federal government.

Congressman Jack Kemp has been pushing for several years now a so-called tax reduction bill (the Kemp-Roth Bill). I support this bill since I believe that any form of tax reduction under any circumstances must eventually bring pressure to bear to cut spending. Moreover, I believe some taxes do more harm than others. There is no doubt that the method by which we collect taxes could be rearranged so as to have a less adverse effect on incentives and production. And, from this point of view, the Kemp-Roth Bill is certainly desirable. We should be clear, however, that it is in reality not a tax reduction bill; it is a proposal to change the form of taxes. As long as high government spending remains, we shall have the hidden tax of inflation. The only true tax cutting proposal would be a proposal to cut government spending. To my knowledge, no one in Washington has yet proposed a genuine tax cutting bill, not President Carter, not the Democrats in Congress, not the Republicans. Every single so-called "tax cut plan" still envisions a higher level of government spending next year and consequently a higher level of taxes, both overt and covert.

There is an important point that needs to be stressed to those who regard themselves as fiscal conservatives. By concentrating on the wrong thing, the deficit, instead of the right thing, total government spending, fiscal conservatives have been the unwitting handmaidens of the big spenders. The typical historical process is that the spenders put through laws which increase government spending. A deficit emerges. The fiscal conservatives scratch their heads and say, "My God, that's terrible; we have got to do something about that deficit." So they cooperate with the big spenders in getting taxes imposed. As soon as the new taxes are imposed and passed, the big spenders are off again, and then there is another burst in government spending and another deficit.

The true cost of government to the public is not measured by explicit taxes but by government spending. If government spends $500 billion, and takes in through taxes $440 billion, which are the approximate figures of President Carter's estimated budget, who pays the difference? Not Santa Claus, but the U.S. citizen. The deficit must be financed by creating money or by borrowing from the public. If it's financed by printing money, that imposes the hidden tax of inflation in addition to the explicit tax. If it's financed by borrowing, then the government gets those resources instead of the private sector. In addition, there will have to be a higher level of taxes in the future to pay the interest or to pay back that debt. Essentially every current piece of wealth in the United States has a hidden tax imposed on it because of the future obligation to pay those extra taxes. In effect, what you have are two kinds of taxes: the open, explicit taxes and the hidden taxes. And what's called a deficit is a hidden tax.

I would far rather have total federal spenidng at $200 billion with a deficit of $100 billion than a balancved budget at $500 billion. The thing we must keep our eye on is what government spends. That's the measure of the amount of the resources of the nation that people cannot individually and separately decide about. It's a measure of the amount we turn over to the bureaucrats to spend on our behalf. I believe along with Parkinson that government will spend whatever the tax system will raise plus a good deal more. Every step we take to strengthen the tax system, whether by getting people to accept payroll taxes they otherwise would not accept, or by cooperating in enacting higher income taxes and excise taxes or whatnot, fosters a higher level of government spending. That's why I am in favor of cutting taxes under any circumstances, for whatever excuse, for whatever reason.

Tax Limitation Laws Are Stopgaps

We have to bear in mind that tax limitation laws are not curealls; they are temporary stopgaps. They are a way of trying to hold back the tide, until public opinion moves in the direction that those of us who believe in limited government hold to be desirable. Without the support of public opinion all the written laws or constitutions you can think of are fundamentally worthless. One has only to look at the results of trying to transplant versions of the American and British constitutions to other nations around the world. I believe, however, that there is a definite movement in public opinion toward greater skepticism of large-scale government programs. People are aware that they are not getting their money's worth through government spendng. Among intellectuals, more and more scholars are coming to the conclusion that many government programs have not had the results intended by their supporters. In journals read by opinion-leaders (for instance, *Commentary, Encounter, Harper's, The Public Interest, The Washington Monthly*), this view is becoming more and more commonly expressed. However, it takes time for such ideas to be accepted by the politicians whio, after all, are mostly followers and not leaders of public opinion.

Let me give an example of what I mean. For about 150 years since the birth of our government (until about the late 1920s) there was no general tendency for government spending to get out of hand. Despite the fact that the same pressures inherent in representative democracy were present through this period, state, local and federal spending was still about 10 percent of national income. For the past 40 years, however, there has been a considerable change in these percentages, to say the least. Except for the Income Tax Amendment, the constitutioal provisions relating to the financing of government were seentially the same as they were in 1789 (and the income tax rate was quite low during this period). The essential difference was that before 1930 or so there was a widespread belief on the part of the public that government should be limited and that danger arose from the growth of government. President Grover Cleveland maintained, for instance, that while the people should support their government, the government should not support the people. President Woodrow Wilson remarked that the history of liberalism was the history of restraints on government power. Almost everyone then agreed that the role of government was to act as a referee and umpire and not as a Big Brother. Once this fundamental attitude of the public changed, however, constitutional restrictions became very much less effective against the growth of government. As we all know, the Supreme Court does follow the election returns (sometimes tardily) and most of the New Deal measures which were ruled unconstitutional by the Court in President Roosevelt's first administration were ruled to be constitutional in the second administration.

The interstate commerce clause as an excuse for federal action is a good case in point. At one time in our history there were transactions which were retarded by the Court and Congress as *intrastate* commerce, but it would take a very ingenious man today to find any transaction whatsoever that the Supreme Court would not declare to be part of *interstate* commerce. The federal government, basically as a result of this change in public opinion, is now allowed to take all sorts of actions that would have been held *by the public* to be unconstitutional sixty or a hundreds years ago.

In the same way, I believe that the effectiveness of tax limitation laws will depend upon their acceptance by the great bulk of the public as part of our constitutional tradition.[1] My own view is that we are seeing a genuine trend in support of the basic philosophy that there should be definite limits on government spending; however, I also believe that such trends take time to solidify and in the meantime I regard tax limitation amendments as a stopgap measure to hold back the tide.

1. In addition, they will not by themselves prevent all further government intervention. Many of the worst kinds of government intervention do not involve much spending. Some examples are tariffs, or regulation of industry (ICC, FCC, FPC) or the controls on the price of natural gas which have done such tremendous harm in the energy area. All of those involve government intervention into the economy in which the spending element is very small.

Chapter 3
Monetary Correction*

SYNOPSIS

There is no technical problem about how to end inflation (Section I). The real obstacles are political, not technical.

Ending inflation would deprive government of revenue it now obtains without legislation (Section II). Replacing this revenue will require government to reduce expenditures, raise explicit taxes, or borrow additional sums from the public — all politically unattractive. I do not know any way to avoid this obstacle.

Political obstacles to ending inflation

Ending inflation would also have the side-effect of producing a temporary, though perhaps fairly protracted, period of economic recession or slowdown and of relatively high unemployment. The political will is today lacking to accept that side-effect. Experience suggests that its occurrence would instead produce an over-reaction involving accelerated government spending and monetary growth that in its turn would produce the initial side-effect of an unsustainable boom followed by accelerated inflation. These side-effects of changes in the rate of inflation arise because of the time it takes for the community to adjust itself to changed rates of growth of spending. The time-delay distorts relative prices, the structure of production and the level of employment. In turn, it takes time to correct these distortions (Section III).

The side-effects of changes in the rate of inflation can be substantially reduced by encouraging the widespread use of price escalator clauses in private and governmental contracts. Such arrangements involve deliberately eschewing some of the advantages of the use of money and hence are not good in and of themselves. They are simply a lesser evil than a badly-managed money. The widespread use of escalator clauses would not by itself either increase or decrease the rate of inflation. But it would reduce the revenue that government acquires from inflation — which also means that government would have less incentive to inflate. More

*Reprinted from Occasional Paper 41, Institute of Economic Affairs 1974. Originally reprinted from the July 1974 issue of FORTUNE Magazine by special permission: © 1974 Time Inc.

important, it would reduce the initial adverse side-effects on output and employment of effective measures to end inflation (Section IV).

Legal enforcement

The use of escalator clauses in government contracts — taxation, borrowing, hiring, purchasing — should be required by law. Their use in private contracts should be permitted and enforceable at law but should be voluntary. The two are related because government adoption of escalator clauses, particularly in taxes, would remove serious impediments to their private adoption (Section V).

Objections to widespread escalation mostly reflect misconceptions about its effects. These misconceptions reflect the same confusion between relative prices and absolute prices that is responsible for many of the adverse effects of accelerated inflation or deflation and for misconceptions about the cause and cure of inflation (Section VI).

I
THE TECHNICAL CAUSE AND CURE OF INFLATION

Short-run changes in both particular prices and in the general level of prices may have many sources. But long-continued inflation is always and everywhere a monetary phenomenon that arises from a more rapid expansion in the quantity of money that in total output[1] — though I hasten to add that the exact rate of inflation is not precisely or mechanically linked to the exact rate of monetary growth. The accompanying Chart (p. 24) plots consumer prices in Britain and the ratio of the quantity of money to output over the last decade.

This statement is only a first step towards an understanding of the causes of any particular inflation. It must be completed by an explanation of the reason for the rapid monetary growth. The

---

[1]This is a bit of an over-simplification, because a fully defensible statement would have to allow for autonomous changes in velocity, i.e., in the demand for real balances, and would have to specify the precise definition of 'money'. But I know of no case in which these qualifications are of critical importance.

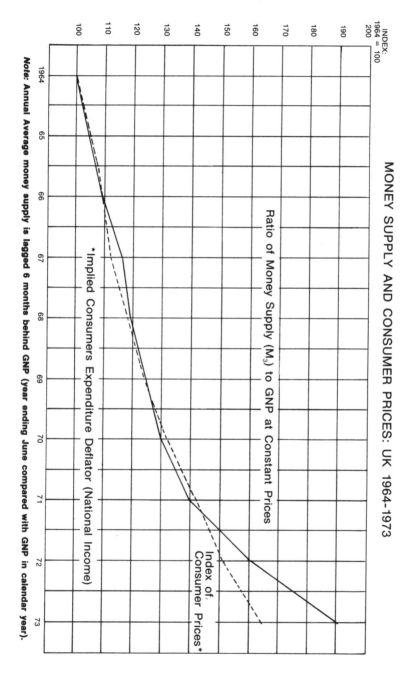

MONEY SUPPLY AND CONSUMER PRICES: UK 1964-1973

Ratio of Money Supply (M₃) to GNP at Constant Prices

*Implied Consumers Expenditure Deflator (National Income)

Index of, Consumer Prices*

INDEX: 1964 = 100

Note: Annual Average money supply is lagged 6 months behind GNP (year ending June compared with GNP in calendar year).

rapid monetary growth that produced inflation in the USA from 1848 to 1860 reflected gold discoveries in California. The rapid monetary growth that produced world inflation from 1890 to 1914 reflected the perfection of the cyanide process for extracting gold from low-grade ore. The rapid monetary growth that has time and again produced wartime inflation has reflected the use of the printing press or its equivalent to finance wartime government spending.

Causes of world-wide growth of money supply

Under modern conditions, the quantity of money is determined by governmental monetary authorities. The accelerated increase in the quantity of money throughout the world in the past decade, which is responsible for the recent acceleration of inflation, has reflected a number of causes:

(1) the attempt to maintain fixed exchange rates, which induced some countries, notably Germany and Japan, to 'import' inflation from the USA;

(2) the expansion in the role of government, and the reluctance to impose explicit taxes, which has induced many governments to use the implicit tax of inflation;

(3) the commitment of governments to a policy of full employment, which has led them to over-react to temporary recessions by measures leading to rapid monetary growth.

Long-continued inflation can be ended only by a reduction in the rate of monetary growth. But, again, this statement is only a first step. The measures that can be used to reduce the rate of monetary growth may vary widely depending on the sources of the excess growth and the institutions of the country in question. For example, if monetary growth has reflected the financing of government expenditures by the printing press, it can be ended by

(a) reducing government spending;

(b) raising taxes;

(c) financing the deficit in the government budget by borrowing from the public rather than by creating money.

But method (c) may not be available for a country that does not have well-developed security markets. And all hyper-inflations have reflected governments so impotent and disorganised as to be unable to employ (b).

Importance — and limitations — of fiscal policy

As these comments imply, fiscal policy may play an important role in producing and curing inflation. Its influence is primarily through its effect on the quantity of money. But its influence can be offset by other forces affecting the quantity of money. Large government surpluses in the USA in 1919 and 1920 did not prevent rapid inflation because they were accompanied by rapid monetary growth which financed private spending. Large government deficits in the USA in 1931 to 1933 did not produce rapid inflation or prevent severe deflation because they were accompanied by a sharp decline in the quantity of money which sharply reduced private spending.

What matters for inflation is not simply the rate of monetary growth but the rate of growth relative to the rate of growth of output, and, in a more sophisticated presentation, relative to the rate of growth in the demand for real money balances at a constant level (or rate of change) of prices. This relationship has led many commentators to emphasise the role of 'productivity', arguing that inflation reflects a decline in productivity (or its rate of growth) and that a cure requires an increase in productivity (or its rate of growth). Though the role of output growth is, in principle, strictly symmetrical to the role of monetary growth, the quantitative orders of magnitude are wholly different. For any given country, over any period longer than a few years, the rate of output growth is unlikely to vary by more than a few percentage points — it would take a major structural change, for example, to raise the rate of growth of output in the USA by two percentage points, from, say, 3-4 per cent per year to 5-6 per cent.[1] On the other hand, the rate of monetary growth can and does vary over a much wider range — it can easily go from 3 or 4 per cent per year to 20 per cent per year. As a matter of experience, therefore,

[1][In the UK the 1970-74 Conservative Government hoped to raise the annual rate of growth from 2.5-3 per cent in the late 1960s to 5 per cent. For a short period in 1972-73 it rose to 6½ per cent (if the official measurements are reliable), but then fell to 4 per cent in 1973. — Ed.]

long-continued inflation is dominated by monetary changes rather than by changes in output.

The importance of the simple proposition in this section is that no measures are likely to produce long-continued inflation or to cure long-continued inflation unless they affect the long-term rate of monetary growth.

II
GOVERNMENT REVENUE FROM INFLATION

Since time immemorial, the major source of inflation has been the sovereign's attempt to acquire resources to wage war, to construct monuments, or for other purposes. Inflation has been irresistibly attractive to sovereigns because it is a hidden tax that at first appears painless or even pleasant, and, above all, because it is a tax that can be imposed without specific legislation. It is truly taxation without representation.

Three ways government gains from inflation

The revenue yield from inflation takes three major forms:

1. Additional government-created fiat money. Since ancient times, sovereigns have debased coinage by replacing silver or gold with base metals.[1] Later, paper currency supplemented token coins. More recently still, book entries at Central Banks (misleadingly called deposits) have been added. Governments use the fiat money that they issue to finance expenditures or repay debt. In addition, the fiat money serves as a base on which the banking system creates additional money in the form of bank deposits.

In the calendar year 1973 the US government realised $8,000 million (£3,300 million) from this source — $6,000 million (£2,500 million) additional currency and coin in circulation on 31 December, 1973 than on 31 December, 1972, and more than

---

[1]One historian of money describes the debasement of the Roman *denarius* from an initially full-bodied silver coin until, by the time of Emperor Diocletian (300 AD), it had become 'practically a copper coin being only slightly washed with silver'. (Rupert J. Ederer, *The Evolution of Money,* Public Affairs Press, Washington, DC, 1964, p. 88.) We have gone further than Diocletian. We wash our copper coins now with nickel, so that not even a trace of silver remains.

$2,000 million (£830 million) in additional deposits at Federal Reserve Banks.[1]

2. Inflation increases the yield of the personal and corporate income tax by pushing individuals and corporations into higher income groups, generating artificial (paper) capital gains on which taxes must be paid, and rendering permitted depreciation allowances inadequate to replace capital, so taxing a return *of* capital to shareholders as if it were a return *on* capital. For the corporation tax alone, the US government realised in 1973 nearly $13,000 million (£5,420 million) from this source.[2]

3. The reduction in the real amount of outstanding National Debt. Much of this debt was issued at yields that did not allow for current rates of inflation. On a conservative estimate, the US government realised in 1973 something like $5,000 million (£2,000 million) from this source.[3]

All told, the US government's revenue from inflation totalled more than $25,000 million (£10,000 million) in 1973. Ending inflation would end this source of revenue. Government would have to reduce expenditures, increase explicit taxes, or borrow additional funds from the public at whatever interest rate would clear the market. None of these courses is politically attractive.

---

[1]Excluding Treasury deposits. Nominally, the Federal Reserve Banks are owned by their member banks. This is a pure formality. In practice the Federal Reserve System is part of the government. It earns 'income' in the form of 'interest' paid to it by the US Treasury on government securities; it returns the excess of such 'interest' over operating expenses to the Treasury. Economic understanding is promoted and confusion avoided by consolidating the accounts of the Federal Reserve System with those of the Treasury.

[2]Inflation produced an over-statement of 1973 corporate profits by more than $26,000 million (£10,800 million) through spurious profits on stocks and under-depreciation, according to Department of Commerce estimates summarised by George Terborgh, *Inflation and Profits,* Machinery and Allied Products Institute (revised, 2 April, 1974). At a 48 per cent corporate tax rate, the additional tax paid was about $12,800 million (£5,300 million). In addition, corporate capital gains were undoubtedly over-stated.

[3]Total interest paid on the roughly $260,000 million (£108,000 million) of Federal debt held by the public was at an average rate of about 5.7 per cent. A 1973 market rate would have been about two percentage points higher, which means that the revenue to the government on this basis was about $5,000 million (£2,000 million). However, in retrospect, it seems clear that 1973 market rates did not adequately allow for inflation.

III
SIDE-EFFECTS ON OUTPUT AND EMPLOYMENT

Acute appendicitis is accompanied by a high fever; the removal of the appendix will require that the patient stay in bed for some days. But the fever is not the cause of the appendicitis and bed-rest is not the cure. Both are side-effects.

The analogy with inflation is striking. The boom that typically accompanies the onset of accelerated inflation is not the cause of the inflation but a side-effect; the recession and unemployment that typically accompany the reduction of inflation are not the cure but a side-effect. There are many ways to increase unemployment that would exacerbate inflation rather than cure it.

Time-lags lead to side-effects

Higher inflation reflects an acceleration in the growth rate of total money spending. Ending inflation requires a deceleration in the growth rate of total spending. The reason for the side-effects from such changes in total spending — both the boom which is generally regarded as a desirable side-effect and the recession which is uniformly regarded as an undesirable side-effect — is the time-delay between an increased or decreased rate of growth of total money spending and the full adjustment of output and prices to that changed rate of growth of total spending.

Essentially the same side-effects will arise whatever may be the cause of the changed growth rate in total spending — just as a high fever accompanies many different diseases and bed-rest many different cures. When non-monetary forces produce brief fluctuations in the rate of growth of total spending, the same side-effects occur. Also, if there is some cause other than unduly rapid monetary growth for long-continued inflation, or some cure other than reduced monetary growth, that cause and that cure will operate largely by affecting the growth rate in total money spending, and hence will produce much the same side-effects. Similarly, the measures proposed later to reduce the adverse side-effects of ending inflation will be effective whatever the cause and whatever the cure.

Hence the rest of this essay is relevant even if you do not accept my monetarist view as expressed in Section I.

Expectations slow to change

When total spending slows down, each producer separately tends to regard the reduction in the demand for his product as special to him, and to hope that it is temporary. He is inclined to meet it primarily by reducing output or accumulating stock, not by shading prices. Only after a time-lag will he start to shade prices. Similarly, any of his workers who are laid off are likely to react by waiting to be recalled or by seeking jobs elsewhere, not by moderating wage demands or expectations. A slowdown in total spending will therefore tend to be reflected initially in a widespread slowdown in output and employment and an increase in stocks. It will take some time before these responses lead in turn to widespread reductions in the rate of inflation and the rate of increase in wages. It will take still more time before *expectations* about inflation are revised and the revised expectations encourage a resumption of employment and output.

This is a highly simplified picture. Different activities have different time-speeds of adjustment. Some prices, wages and production schedules are fixed a long time in advance; others can be adjusted promptly. As a result, a slowdown of total spending produces substantial shifts in *relative* prices, which will sooner or later have to be corrected; the correction in turn will cause economic disturbances.

For the USA, study of monetary history[1] indicates that the time-delay between a change in the rate of monetary growth and a corresponding change in the rate of growth of total spending and total output has averaged six to nine months; between the change in the rate of growth of spending and of prices, 12 to 18 months. Accordingly, the total delay between a change in monetary growth and in the rate of inflation has been about two years.[2] For the UK, the available evidence indicates that the time-delay is roughly the same as for the USA.

[1] Milton Friedman, *The Optimum Quantity of Money,* Macmillan, London, 1969, Chapters 10, 11 and 12, and 'Letter on Monetary Policy', *Review,* Federal Reserve Bank of Saint Louis, March 1974. Also, A. James Meigs, *Money Matters,* Harper and Row, New York, 1972, Chapter 6.

[2] This is precisely what W. Stanley Jevons estimated it to be: 'An expansion of the currency occurs one or two years prior to a rise of prices.' *(Investigations into Currency and Finance,* Macmillan, 1884, p. 107.)

Serious effects on lending

The time-delay and resultant distortion are particularly clear for loans, where the distinction between *nominal* and *real* is especially important. Suppose you lend someone £100 in return for a promise to pay you £110 a year later. Neglect any possibility of default. What interest rate have you received? In pounds, 10 per cent. But if prices have risen by 10 per cent during the year, the £110 will buy only as much as the £100 would have done a year earlier. Your *real* return is nil. Indeed, if, as is true today, the £10 nominal return is subject to income tax, your *real* return is negative. You end up with *less* than you started with.

If you entered into a mortgage some years back, you may have paid 5 or 6 per cent. Given the inflation of the past few years, your effective *real* rate may have been nil. The rising price level probably raised the value of your property by as much as, or more than, the interest you paid. The lender in turn received a *real* return of nil—or a negative return if he was liable to tax. Similarly, consider someone who today takes out a mortgage at 11 per cent or more. Suppose economic policy were successful in bringing inflation down to nil. He would be in severe difficulties (unless of course the rate were reduced), and the lender would have received a wholly unexpected gain.

Failure of political will

Such side-effects constitute, I believe, the most important political obstacle to ending inflation, given, first, the commitment on the part of the US, UK and most other governments to 'full employment', secondly the failure of the public at large to recognise the inevitable if temporary side-effects of ending inflation, and thirdly, the unwillingness or inability of political leaders to persuade the public to accept these side-effects.

Some years ago, when inflation was much lower than now, I believed that the re-adjustment required was sufficiently mild and brief to be politically feasible. But unfortunately in the USA the opportunity was cast aside on 15 August, 1971, when President Nixon reversed economic policy by imposing a price and wage freeze and encouraging expansive monetary and fiscal policy. At the time, we were well on the way to ending inflation without severe side-effects. At the cost of the mild 1970 recession, the annual rate of inflation had been reduced from over 6 per cent to 4.5 per cent and was still declining. The economy was slowly recovering from that recession. Had the nation had the will—for President Nixon was reflecting a widespread national consensus when he reversed policy—another year of continued monetary restraint and of slow expansion would probably have turned the trick. As it was, the 1970 recession was a masochistic exercise rather than a side-effect of a successful cure.

Inflation in the USA is currently (mid-1974) far worse than in August 1971. The 14 per cent rate in the first quarter of 1974 was doubtless a temporary bubble, but, even on the most optimistic view, inflation is not likely to fall below 6 per cent during the coming year. Starting from that level, and with inflationary expectations even more deeply entrenched, an effective policy to end inflation would entail as a side-effect a considerably more severe and protracted recession than we experienced in 1970. The political will to accept such a recession, without reversing policy and re-stimulating inflation, is simply not present.

What then? If we—and probably Britain and other countries similarly placed—do nothing, we shall suffer even higher rates of inflation—not continuously, but in spurts as we over-react to temporary recessions. Sooner or later, the public will get fed up, will demand effective action, and we shall then have a really severe recession.

IV
EASING THE SIDE-EFFECTS

How can we make it politically feasible to end inflation much sooner? As I see it, inflation can be ended sooner only by adopting measures that will reduce the side-effects from ending it. These side-effects fundamentally reflect distortions introduced into *relative* prices by *unanticipated* inflation or deflation, distortions that arise because contracts are entered into in terms of *nominal* prices under mistaken perceptions about the likely course of inflation.

Escalator clauses: an illustration

The way to reduce these side-effects is to make contracts in *real*, not nominal, terms. This can be done by the widespread use of escalator clauses.

Let me illustrate. In 1967 General Motors and the United Automobile Workers Union reached a wage agreement for a three-year period. At the time, prices had been relatively stable, consumer prices having risen at the average rate of 2.5 per cent in the preceding three years. The wage agreement was presumably based on an expectation by both General Motors and the union that prices would continue to rise at 2.5 per cent or less. That expectation was not realised. From 1967 to 1970, prices rose at an average annual rate of 5.2 per cent. The result was that General Motors paid *real* wages that were increasingly lower than the levels both parties had expected. The unexpected fall in real wages was a stimulus to General Motors, and no doubt led it to produce at a higher rate than otherwise. Initially, the unexpected fall in real wages was no deterrent to workers, since it took some time before they recognised that the accelerated rise in consumer prices was more than a transitory phenomenon. But by 1970 they were certainly aware that their real wages were less than they had bargained for.

The result was a strike in late 1970, settled by a wage agreement that provided (1) a very large increase in the initial year; (2) much smaller increases for the next two years; and (3) a cost-of-living escalator clause.

The contract was widely characterised as 'inflationary'. It was no such thing. The large initial year increase simply made up for the effect of the past unanticipated inflation. It restored *real wages* to the levels at which both parties had expected them to be. The escalator clause was designed to prevent a future similar distortion, and it has done so.

This General Motors example illustrates a side-effect of unanticipated inflation. Suppose the same contract had been reached in 1967 but that the rate of inflation, instead of accelerating, had declined from 2.5 per cent to nil. Real wages would then have risen about the level both parties had anticipated; General Motors would have been driven to reduce output and employment; the workers would have welcomed the unexpectedly high real wage-rate but would have deplored the lower employment; when contract renewal was due, the union, not General Motors, would have been in a weak bargaining position.

An escalator clause which works both up and down would have prevented both the actual side-effects from unanticipated inflation and the hypothetical side-effects from unanticipated deflation. It would have enabled employers and employees to bargain in terms of the conditions of their own industry without having also to guess what was going to happen to prices in general, because both General Motors and the union would have been protected against either more rapid inflation or less rapid inflation.

Useful though they are, widespread escalator clauses are not a panacea. It is impossible to escalate *all* contracts (consider, for example, paper currency), and costly to escalate many. A powerful advantage of using money is precisely the ability to carry on transactions cheaply and efficiently, and universal escalator clauses reduce this advantage. Far better to have no inflation and no escalator clauses. But that alternative is not currently available.

Origins of the escalator: the 'tabular standard'

Let me note also that the widespread use of escalator clauses is not a new or untried idea. It dates back to at least 1707, when a Cambridge don, William Fleetwood, estimated the change in prices over a 600-year period in order to calculate comparable limits on outside income that college Fellows were permitted to receive. It was suggested explicitly in 1807 by an English writer on money, John Wheatley. It was spelled out in considerable detail and recommended enthusiastically in 1886 by the great English economist, Alfred Marshall. The great American economist Irving Fisher not only favoured the 'tabular standard'—as the proposal for widespread indexation was labelled nearly two centuries ago—but also persuaded a manufacturing company that he helped to found to issue a purchasing-power security as long ago as 1925. Interest in the 'tabular standard' was the major factor accounting for the development of index numbers of prices. In recent years, the 'tabular standard' has been adopted by Brazil on a wider scale than I would recommend for the USA. It has been adopted on a smaller scale by Canada, Israel, and many other countries.

V

THE SPECIFIC PROPOSAL

For the USA, my specific proposal has two parts, one for the Federal government, one for the rest of the economy. For the Federal government, I propose that escalator clauses be legislated; for the rest of the economy, that they be voluntary but that any legal obstacles be removed. The question of which index number to use in such escalator clauses is important but not critical. As Alfred Marshall said in 1886, 'A perfectly exact measure of purchasing power is not only unattainable, but even unthinkable'. For the USA, as a matter of convenience, I would use the cost-of-living index number calculated by the Bureau of Labour Statistics.

(a) The Government

The US government has already adopted escalation for social security payments, retirement benefits to Federal employees, wages of many government employees, and perhaps some other items. Taxes which are expressed as fixed percentages of price or other value base are escalated automatically. The key additional requirement is for escalator clauses in the personal and corporate income tax and in government securities.

The personal tax. Minor details aside, four revisions are called for:

 (i) The personal exemption, the standard deduction, and the low income question to the index for the base year in which 'indexation' starts. For example, if in the first year prices rise by 10 per cent, then the present amounts should be multiplied by 110/100 or 1.10.

 (ii) The brackets in the tax tables should be adjusted similarly, so that, in the examples given, 0-$500 would become 0-$550, and so on.

   (These two measures have been adopted by Canada.)

(iii) The base for calculating capital gains should be multiplied by the ratio of the price index in the year of sale to the price index in the year of purchase. This would prevent the taxing of non-existent, purely paper capital gains.

(iv) The base for calculating depreciation on fixed capital assets should be adjusted in the same way as the base for calculating capital gains.

The corporate tax.[1]

(i) The present $25,000 (£10,400) dividing line between normal tax and surtax should be replaced by that sum multiplied by a price index number.

(ii) The cost of stocks used in sales should be adjusted to eliminate book profits (or losses) resulting from changes in prices between initial purchase and final sale.

The base for calculating (iii) capital gains, and (iv) depreciation of fixed capital assets should be adjusted as for the personal tax.

Government securities[1] Except for short-term bills and notes, all government securities should be issued in purchasing-power form. (For example, Series E bonds should promise a redemption value equal to the product of the face value calculated at, say, 3 per cent per year and the ratio of the price index in the year of redemption to the price index in the year of purchase.) Coupon securities should carry coupons redeemable for the face amount multiplied by the relevant price ratio, and bear a maturity value equal to the face amount similarly multiplied by the relevant price ratio.

These changes in taxes and in borrowing would reduce both the incentive for government to resort to inflation and the side-effects of changes in the rate of inflation on the private economy. But they are called for also by elementary principles of ethics, justice, and representative government, which is why I propose making them permanent.

Taxation inflated to record levels

As a result largely of inflation produced by government in the USA, the UK and elsewhere, personal income taxes are today heavier than during the peak of Second World War financing,

---

[1]These tax and borrowing measures are all contained in a Bill introduced by Senator James Buckley in April 1974.

despite several 'reductions' in tax rates. Personal exemptions in real terms are at a record low level. The taxes levied on persons in different economic circumstances deviate widely from the taxes explicitly intended to apply to them. Government has been in the enviable position of imposing higher taxes while appearing to reduce taxes. The less enviable result has been a wholly arbitrary distribution of the higher taxes.

As for government borrowing, the savings bond campaigns of the US and UK Treasuries have been the largest bucket-shop operations ever engaged in.[1] This is not a recent development. In responding to a questionnaire of the Joint Economic Committee of Congress, I wrote as early as 1951:

'I strongly favour the issuance of a purchasing-power bond on two grounds: (a) It would provide a means for lower- and middle-income groups to protect their capital against the ravages of inflation. This group has almost no effective means of doing so now. It seems to me equitable and socially desirable that they should. (b) It would permit the Treasury to sell bonds without engaging in advertising and promotion that at best is highly misleading, at worst, close to being downright immoral. The Treasury urges people to buy bonds as a means of securing their future. Is the implicit promise one that it can make in good faith, in light of past experience of purchasers of such bonds who have seen their purchasing power eaten away by price rises? If it can be, there is no cost involved in making the promise explicit by adding a purchasing-power guarantee. If it cannot be, it seems to me intolerable that an agency of the public deliberately mislead the public.'

Surely the experience of the nearly quarter-century since these words were written reinforces their pertinence. Essentially

[1] [In the UK the *Report* of the Committee to Review National Savings (the Page Committee: Cmnd. 5273, HMSO, June 1973) found that 'the £9,546 million of National Savings invested at the end of March 1972 was worth only £4,269 million if expressed in the purchasing power of money in March 1951. Since the total value of National Savings at end March 1951 was £6,130 million, in real terms National Savings are contracting' (para. 568). It therefore examined the arguments for and against index-linking for government securities and concluded that 'an experiment should be undertaken of issuing a modest index-linked bond for the small saver on the grounds that he is least able to protect his capital against inflation' (para. 583). — Ed.]

every purchaser of savings bonds or, indeed, almost any other long-term Treasury security during that period, has paid for the privilege of lending to the government: the supposed 'interest' he has received has not compensated for the decline in the purchasing power of the principal, and, to add insult to injury, he has had to pay tax on the paper interest. And the inflation which has sheared the innocent lambs has been produced by the government which benefits from the shearing.

It is a mystery to me — and a depressing commentary on either the understanding or the sense of social responsibility of businessmen (I say business *men*, not business) — that year after year eminent and honourable business leaders have been willing to aid and abet this bucket-shop operation by joining committees to promote the sale of US saving bonds or by providing facilities for payroll deductions for their employees who buy them.

(b) The Private Economy

Private use of escalator clauses is an expedient that has no permanent role, if government manages money responsibly. Hence I favour keeping private use voluntary in order to promote its self-destruction if that happy event arrives.

No legislation is required for the private adoption of escalator clauses, which are now widespread. Something over 5 million US workers[1] are covered by union contracts with automatic escalator clauses, and there must be many non-union workers who have similar implicit or explicit agreements with their employers. Many contracts for future delivery of products contain provisions for adjustment of the final selling price either for specific changes in costs or for general price changes. Many rental contracts for business premises are expressed as a percentage of gross or net receipts, which means that they have an implicit escalator clause. This is equally true for percentage royalty payments and for automobile insurance policies that pay the cost of repairing damage. Some insurance companies issue fire insurance policies the face

---

[1] [Eight to nine million in the UK where threshold agreements have been widely adopted since they received the Conservative Government's sanction in its counter-inflation policy: *The price and pay code for Stage 3. A consultative document*, Cmnd. 5444, HMSO, Autumn 1973. — Ed.]

value of which is automatically adjusted for inflation. No doubt there are many more examples of which I am ignorant.

It is highly desirable that escalator clauses should be incorporated in a far wider range of wage agreements, contracts for future delivery of products, and financial transactions involving borrowing and lending. The first two are entirely straightforward extensions of existing practices. The third is more novel.

'Indexation' for corporate loans

The arrangements suggested for government borrowings would apply equally to long-term borrowing by private enterprises. Instead of issuing a security promising to pay, say, interest of 9 per cent per year and to repay £1,000 at the end of five years, the XYZ company could promise to pay 3 per cent plus the rate of inflation each year and to repay £1,000 at the end of five years. Alternatively, it could promise to pay each year 3 per cent times the ratio of the price index in that year to the price index in the year the security was issued and to repay at the end of five years £1,000 times the corresponding price ratio for the fifth year. (The alternative methods are illustrated in Table I.) If there is inflation, the first method implicitly involves amortising part of the real value of the bond over the five-year period; the second involves currently paying interest only, at a constant real rate, and repaying the whole principal in *real* value at the end of the five years.

TABLE I

Hypothetical Indexed Bond

£1,000 five-year bond issued in 1968 at a real rate of 3 per cent

Year	UK Consumer Index (1968=100)	Price Level Percentage change	Method 1 Interest	Method 2 Interest
			£	£
1968	100			
1969	105.2	5.2	82	31.56
1970	112.0	6.5	95	33.60
1971	122.6	9.5	125	36.78
1972	131.0	6.8	98	39.60
1973	142.0	8.4	114	42.60
			Principal	
			£1,000	£1,420

So far, there has been little incentive for private borrowers to issue such securities. The delay in adjusting anticipations about inflation to the actual acceleration of inflation has meant that interest rates on long-term bonds have been extremely low in real terms. Almost all enterprises that have issued bonds in the past decade have done extremely well—the rate of inflation has often exceeded the interest rate they had to pay, making the real cost negative.

Lenders' changing expectations

Three factors could change this situation.

(1) As lenders, who have been the losers so far, come to have more accurate expectations of inflation, borrowers will have to pay rates high enough to compensate for the actual inflation.

(2) Government purchasing-power securities might prove so attractive that competition would force private enterprises to do the same.

(3) Related to (2), if it became clear that there was a real possibility that government would follow effective policies to stem inflation, borrowing would no longer be a one-way street. Enterprises would become concerned that they might become locked into high-interest rate loans. They might then have more interest in protecting themselves against inflation.

Businessmen's fears unwarranted

One question has invariably been raised when I have discussed this possibility with corporate executives: 'Is it not too risky for us to undertake an open-ended commitment? At least with fixed nominal rates we know what our obligations are'. This is a natural query from business men reared in an environment in which a roughly stable price level was taken for granted. But in a world of *varying* rates of inflation, the *fixed*-rate agreement is the more risky agreement. To quote Alfred Marshall again,

> 'Once it [the tabular standard] has become familiar none but gamblers would lend or borrow on any other terms, at all events for long periods.'

The money receipts of most businesses vary with inflation. If inflation is high, their receipts in money terms are high and they can pay the escalated rate of interest; if inflation is low, their receipts are low and they will find it easier to pay the low rate with the adjustment for inflation than a fixed but high rate; and similarly at the time of redemption.

The crucial point is the relation between assets and liabilities. Currently, for many enterprises, their assets, including goodwill, are real in the sense that their money value will rise or fall with the general price level; but their liabilities tend to be nominal, i.e. fixed in money terms. Accordingly, these enterprises benefit from inflation at a higher rate than was anticipated when the nominal liabilities were acquired and are harmed by inflation at a lower rate than was anticipated. If assets and liabilities were to match, such enterprises would be protected against either event.

Home mortgages—threat of 'major crisis'

A related yet somewhat different case is provided by financial intermediaries. Consider savings and loan associations and mutual savings banks. Both their assets (primarily home mortgages) and their liabilities (due to shareholders or depositors) are expressed in money terms. But they differ in time duration. The liabilities are in practice due on demand;[1] the assets are long-term. The current mortgages were mostly issued when inflation, and therefore interest rates, were much lower than they are now. If the mortgages were re-valued at current yields, i.e. at the market prices for which they could be sold in a free secondary market, every US savings and loan association would be technically insolvent.

So long as the thrift institutions can maintain their level of deposits, no problem arises because they do not have to liquidate their assets. But if inflation speeds up, interest rates on market instruments will rise further. Unless the thrift institutions offer competitive interest rates, their shareholders or depositors will withdraw funds to get a better yield (the process inelegantly termed 'disintermediation'). But with their income fixed, the thrift

[1][Or, in Britain, at short notice. — Ed.]

institutions will find it difficult or impossible to pay competitive rates. This situation is concealed but not altered by the legal limits on the rates they are permitted to pay.

Further acceleration of inflation threatens a major crisis for this group of financial institutions. And the crisis is no minor matter. Total assets of these US institutions approach $400,000 million (£167,000 million).[1] As it happens, they would be greatly helped by a deceleration of inflation, but some of their recent borrowers who are locked into high rates on mortgages would be seriously hurt.[2]

Benefits of inflation-proofed loans

Consider how different the situation of the thrift institutions would be with widespread escalator clauses: the mortgages on their books would be yielding, say, 5 per cent plus the rate of inflation; they could afford to pay their shareholders or depositors, say, 3 or 4 per cent plus the rate of inflation. They, their borrowers, and their shareholders or depositors wold be fully protected against changes in the rate of inflation. They would be assuming risks only with respect to the much smaller possible changes in the *real* rate or interest rather than in the money rate.

Similarly an insurance company could afford to offer an inflation-protected policy if its assets were in inflation-protected loans to business or in mortgages or government securities. A pension fund could offer inflation-protected pensions if it held inflation-protected assets. In Brazil, where this practice has, to my knowledge, been carried furthest, banks are required to credit a 'monetary correction' equal to the rate of inflation on all time deposits and to charge a 'monetary correction' on all loans extending beyond some minimum period.

To repeat, none of these arrangements is without cost. It would be far better if stable prices made them unnecessary. But they seem to me far less costly than continuing on the road to periodic acceleration of inflation, ending in a real bust.

[1] [British building society assets exceed £17,500 million. — Ed.]

[2] [Unless interest rates are lowered, as they would be in Britain. — Ed.]

The suggested governmental arrangements would stimulate the private arrangements. Today, one deterrent to issuing private purchasing-power securities is that the inflation adjustment would be taxable to the recipient along with the real interest paid. The proposed tax changes would in effect exempt such adjustments from taxation, and so make purchasing-power securities more attractive to lenders. In addition, government issues of purchasing-power securities would offer effective competition to private borrowers, inducing them to follow suit, and would provide assets that could be used as the counterpart of inflation-protected liabilities.

Prospects for private contract escalators

Would escalator clauses spread in private contracts? That depends on the course of inflation. If, by some miracle, inflation were to disappear in the near future, all talk of such arrangements would also disappear. The more likely development is that US inflation will taper off in late 1974, will settle at something like 6 or 7 per cent in 1975, and will then start to accelerate in 1976 in response to the delayed impact of over-reaction in 1974 to rising unemployment. During this period there will be a steady but unspectacular expansion of escalator clauses. If inflation accelerates to 10 per cent and beyond in 1977 or so, the steady expansion will turn into a bandwagon.

Needless to say, I hope this scenario is wrong. I hope that the Federal Reserve and the Administration will be willing and able to resist the pressure to over-react to the 1974 recession, that they will maintain fiscal and monetary restraint, and so avoid another acceleration of inflation. But neither past experience, nor the present political climate, makes that hope a reasonable expectation.

Making it easier to fight inflation

How would widespread adoption of the escalator principle affect economic policy? Some critics say indexation would condemn us to perpetual inflation. I believe that, on the contrary, indexation would enhance government's ability to act against inflation.

To begin with, indexation will temper some of the hardships and distortions that now follow from a drop in the rate of inflation. Employers will not be stuck with excessively high wage increases under existing union contracts, for wage increases will moderate as inflation recedes. Borrowers will not be stuck with excessively high interest costs, for the rates on outstanding loans will moderate as inflation recedes. Indexation will also partly counteract the tendency of business to defer capital investment once total spending begins to decline — there will be less reason to wait in expectation of lower prices and lower interest rates. Businesses will be able to borrow funds or enter into construction contracts knowing that interest rates and contract prices will be adjusted later in accord with indexes of prices.

Most important, indexation will shorten the time it takes for a reduction in the rate of growth of total spending to have its full effect in reducing the rate of inflation. As the deceleration of demand pinches at various points in the economy, any effects on prices will be transmitted promptly to wage contracts, contracts for future delivery, and interest rates on outstanding long-term loans. Accordingly, producers' wage costs and other costs will go up less rapidly than they would without indexation. This tempering of costs, in turn, will encourage employers to keep more people on the payroll, and produce more goods, than they would without indexation. The encouragement of supply, in turn, will work against price increases, with additional moderating feedback on wages and other costs.

With widespread indexation, in sum, firm monetary restraint by the Federal Reserve System (the 'Fed') would be reflected in a much more even reduction in the pace of inflation and a much smaller transitory rise in unemployment. The success in slowing inflation would steel political will to suffer the smaller withdrawal pains and so might make it possible for the 'Fed' to persist in a firm policy. As it became credible that the 'Fed' would persist, private reactions could reinforce the effects of its policy. The economy would move to non-inflationary growth at high levels of employment much more rapidly than now seems possible.

VI
OBJECTIONS TO ESCALATOR CLAUSES

The major objection to widespread escalation is the allegation that escalators have an inflationary impact on the economy[1] In this simple-minded form, the statement is simply false — as I noted earlier in connection with the 1970 General Motors settlement. An escalator goes into effect only as the *result* of a *previous* price increase. Whence came that? An escalator can go down as well as up. If inflation slows, and hence so do wage increases, do escalators have a *deflationary* impact?

In the first instance, escalators have *no* direct effect on the rate of inflation. They simply assure that inflation affects different prices and wages alike and thus avoid the kind of distortions in relative prices and wages illustrated by the General Motors case. With widespread escalation, inflation would be *transmitted* more quickly and evenly, and hence the harm done by inflation would be less. But why should that raise or lower the *rate* of inflation?

Incentive to raise tax rates?

Two objections have been made on a more sophisticated level. First, widespread escalation would restrict the government revenue from inflation simply to the direct tax on cash balances produced by the issue of additional high-powered money [point (1), p. 27]. It would thereby reduce the revenue from a given rate of inflation, which could induce the government to raise the rate of tax.

'Living with inflation'

Second, the general public could interpret the adoption of escalator clauses as demonstrating that the government has given up the fight against inflation, and is seeking only to 'live with inflation'. This might lead the public to raise its own anticipations of future inflation, which, by reducing its willingness to hold cash balances, could cause a once-for-all rise in the price level and to that extent be a self-fulfilling prophecy.

[1] [A Treasury Minister in the 1970-74 Conservative Government has argued that those who advocate indexation are 'arguing that one ought to try to live with inflation rather than control it, which I regard as a dangerous point from which to start'. (Mr. Terence Higgins, *Hansard*, 20 May, 1974, col. 83.) — Ed.]

Neither objection seems to me weighty. If the public does not wish to stop inflation but is content to allow government to use inflation as a regular source of revenue, the sooner we adapt our institutions to that situation the better. Similarly, the second objection has little relevance to the proposal for escalator clauses as a means for removing *political* obstacles to ending inflation.

On a still more sophisticated level, it can be argued that, by removing distortions in relative prices produced by inflation, widespread escalator clauses would make it easier for the public to recognise changes in the rate of inflation, would thereby reduce the time-lag in adapting to such changes, and thus make the nominal price level more sensitive and variable. This is certainly possible, though by no means demonstrated. But, if so, the *real variables* would be made *less* sensitive and *more* stable — a highly beneficial trade-off. Moreover, it is also possible that, by making accurate estimates of the rate of inflation less important, widespread escalator clauses would reduce the attention devoted to such estimates, and thereby provide more stability.

An objection of a very different kind is that inflation serves the critical social purpose of resolving incompatible demands by different groups. To put it crudely, the participants in the economy have 'non-negotiable demands' for more than the whole output. These demands are reconciled because inflation fools people into believing that their demands have been met when in fact they have not been, nominal returns being eroded by unanticipated inflation.

Escalator clauses, it is argued, bring the inconsistent demands into the open. Workers who would accept a lower real wage produced by unanticipated inflation will not be willing to accept the same real wage in explicit negotiations.[1] If this view is correct on a wide enough scale to be important, I see no ultimate outcome other than either runaway inflation or an authoritarian society ruled by force. Perhaps it is only wishful thinking that makes me reluctant to accept this vision of our fate.

---

[1] [This is essentially the 'money illusion' behind Keynes's view that workers would not accept lower money wages but would accept lower real wages resulting from unchanged (or even rising) money wages reduced in real value by rising prices (inflation). — Ed.]

VII
CONCLUSION

The conventional political wisdom is that the citizenry may mutter about inflation but votes on the basis of the level of unemployment. Nobody, it is said, has ever lost an election because of inflation: Hoover in 1932 and Nixon in 1960 lost because of unemployment.

As we leave the depression decade farther and farther behind, and as we experience more and more inflation, this conventional wisdom becomes increasingly questionable. Inflation surely helped to make Mr. Edward Heath Prime Minister in 1970 and, even more surely, ex-Prime Minister in 1974. The popularity of Japan's Prime Minister, Mr. K. Tanaka, is at an all-time low because of inflation. President Allende of Chile lost his life at least partly because of inflation. Throughout the world, inflation is a major source of political unrest.

Perhaps widespread escalator clauses are not the best expedient in this time of trouble. But I know of no other that has been suggested that holds out as much promise of both reducing the harm done by inflation and facilitating the ending of inflation. If inflation continues to accelerate, the conventional political wisdom will be reversed. The insistence on ending inflation at whatever cost will lead to a severe depression. Now, before that has occurred, is the time to take measures that will make it politically feasible to end inflation before inflation ends not only the conventional wisdom but perhaps also the free society.

Monetary Correction: The British Context

To illustrate the relevance of Professor Friedman's analysis for the British economy we add Charts on the main indicators—Ed.

CHART 1

MONEY SUPPLY: UK

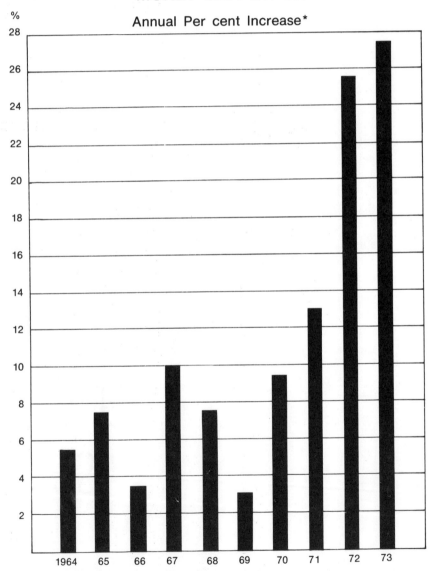

Annual Per cent Increase*

*Increase in Money Stock (M$_3$)

CHART 2

WEEKLY EARNINGS IN INDUSTRY: UK

Annual Per cent Increase

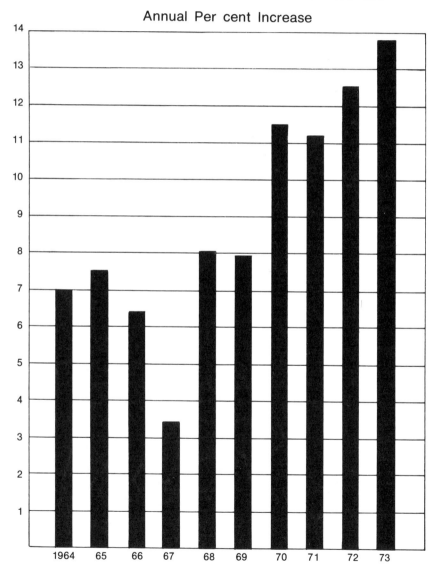

CHART 3

RETAIL PRICES: UK

Annual Per cent Increase 1964-1974

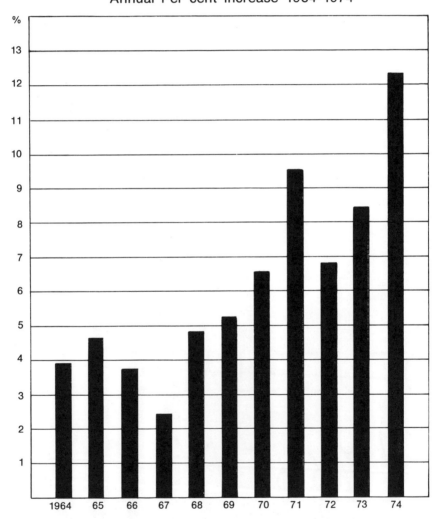

*1st Quarter compared with 1st Quarter 1973

CHART 4
PRICE INCREASE IN UK AND OTHER COUNTRIES
Per cent Increase in Consumer Prices 1970-1973

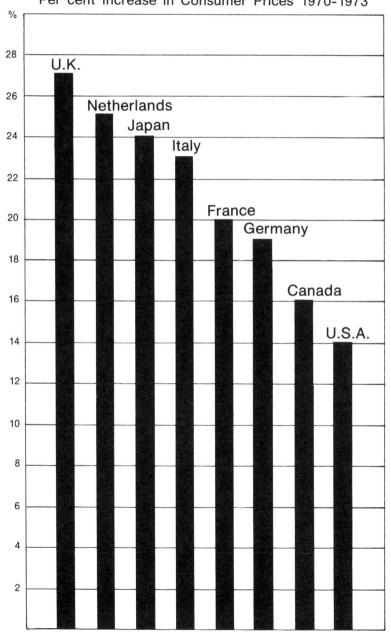

Chapter 4
From Galbraith
To Economic Freedom*

PART I
THE CONVENTIONAL WISDOM OF J. K. GALBRAITH

I
INTRODUCTION

I want to start out by explaining that I have no prejudice against John Kenneth Galbraith. Indeed some of my best friends are Galbraithians, including John Kenneth. I say this because there is often somewhat of a tendency to attribute to motives what is really to be attributed to honest difference of opinion. Galbraith deserves a good deal of credit for his independence of mind, for his diligence in trying to spread and promote his ideas, and for an attempt to put intellectual content into some of them.

I mean that seriously. For example, in one policy which is rather peripheral to his general body of thought, namely that of price and wage control, Kenneth Galbraith has the company of many other people from many other points of view who are in favour of, or have from time to time espoused, wage and price control, but so far as I know, he is the only person who has made a serious attempt to present a theoretical analysis to justify his position, in a book called *A Theory of Price Control*[1] he wrote not long after World War II. I happen to think that the analysis is wrong, but at least it is a serious attempt to provide a basis for a point of view.

There are even some subjects and some issues on which he and I have been in agreement. The most important of those, I think, in the United States setting, was the question of military conscription. Kenneth Galbraith, like me, was for many years a strong and public opponent of military conscription, and this de-

*Reprinted from Occasional Paper 49, Institute of Economic Affairs 1977.
[1] Harvard University Press, Cambridge, Mass., 1952.

spite that some of his closest political allies — for example, Senator Edward Kennedy — were on the other side of the argument. Also, not quite two years ago, when shortly after he became President, Mr. Ford assembled a summit meeting of various groups of people to advise him on inflation, I was fascinated to find that at a meeting of economists Galbraith was one of the few outside of those whom you would expect to take this position — the so-called 'liberal' economists — to take the problem of inflation seriously and to regard it as something which had to be corrected.

II
CONVICTION AND DOCUMENTATION

Having said this, I want to proceed to analyse his thought and his position, but I do so, as I say, with full respect for him as an individual and for his independence. The puzzle I find on reading Galbraith, and the one which will provide something of a theme for what I have to say, is how to reconcile his own sincere *conviction* in the validity of his view of the world with the almost complete failure of any other students — even those who are sympathetic with his general political orientation — to *document* its validity. There have been many people who have looked at his picture of the world, but, although there must be some exceptions, I do not know of any serious scholars who have validated his conception. Kenneth Galbraith has obviously read these criticisms and seen these arguments. The puzzle I want to propose for you is how to reconcile his conviction in the validity of that view with the failure of others to document it.

Affluence for whom?

The typical conventional approach to the conventional wisdom of John Kenneth Galbraith has been to treat him as if he were trying to examine and describe the world and then to compare the position he arrives at with reality. In briefly surveying this conventional approach we may start with *The Affluent Society*,[1] a book, interestingly enough, which was published just before

[1]Hamish Hamilton, 1958; Pelican Books, 1962.

the 'war on poverty' became a widespread obsession. Now I may say I regard that as less of a reflection on Galbraith than on the proponents of the war on poverty. In the fundamental point of view that we are indeed a relatively affluent society, Galbraith was entirely correct. The war on poverty of which so much has been made since then has been a very good thing indeed for many thousands of civil servants who have been able to make excellent careers and many thousands of academic people who have been able to do study after study on poverty. But it has not done very much to help the people who are most disadvantaged in our economy and society.

The main content of the book was not really the affluence of society. Rather it was devoted to other themes: to denigrating the tastes of ordinary people, the tastes of those who prefer pushpin to poetry, who prefer large tailfins to nice, compact, expensive little cars. It was directed to developing the advantages of extending the power of government. A major theme was the alleged contrast between private affluence and public squalor.

In mentioning the criticisms which were made of that theme I must make a start with a review of Galbraith's 1958 *Affluent Society* written by Adam Smith in 1776. I quote from Adam Smith:

'It is the highest impertinence and presumption in kings and ministers to pretend to watch over the economy of private people and to restrain their expense either by sumptuary laws or by prohibiting the importation of foreign luxuries. They are themselves always and without any exception the greatest spendthrifts in the society. Let them look well after their own expenses and they may safely trust private people with theirs. If their own extravagance does not ruin the state, that of their subjects never will.'

So I think most of us would agree that 'public affluence and private penury' comes closer to a correct description of the world. I cannot resist adding another of Smith's devastating comments, not so immediately relevant to Galbraith's book but it is a little.

'There is no art which one government sooner learns of another than that of draining money from the pockets of the people.'

That is an art which certainly your government and my government have learned very well.

The general reaction of his contemporaries was not much different from Adam Smith's reaction. There was widespread criticism of Galbraith's denigration of public attitudes in terms of his being a 'tailfin burner', like the book burner of an earlier day. Who was he to tell people what they should like?

Galbraith and advertising

There was an examination of his animadversions on advertising. You will recall that one of the main themes in *The Affluent Society* was the enormous power which Galbraith assigned to advertising: that these tastes for tailfins were not natural or native, that they were created by greedy producers seeking to shape the tastes of the public to satisfy their own interests. There resulted a considerable expansion in the economic analysis of advertising which tended to demonstrate, first, that a very large fraction of all advertising was informative rather than persuasive, secondly, that even in persuasive advertising the smart and intelligent thing for an enterprise to do was to find out what the public wants and then make it and advise them of it, not to try to shape its tastes. But, more important from Galbraith's general point of view, there was a great deal of emphasis on the extent to which you had advertising not only by private enterprise but also by government and bureaucrats, and that this has at least as widespread an effect as private advertising.

The statistics on government spending made Galbraith's theme of private affluence versus public squalor an absurd claim. Anybody who studies the statistics knows that government spending has grown apace. In the United States it has grown from about 10 per cent of the national income in 1929 to something over 40 per cent today. In the United Kingdom it has grown from 10 per cent of the national income at the time of the Diamond Jubilee of Queen Victoria to something like 60 per cent today. It is very hard, in the face of these figures, to maintain the claim that is the private spendthrifts and not the public spendthrifts who are impoverishing the nation.

Countervailing power — the 'unholy trinity'?

Let me go on from his affluent society to his theory of countervailing power,[1] a book to which George Stigler once addressed a devastating review under the title 'The Economist Plays with Blocs'.[2] The thesis which Galbraith set up in that book was that when concentrations of power arise they stimulate countervailing concentrations of power. Big business stimulates big labour, and both stimulate big government. And the combination of big business, big labour and big government is a holy, not an unholy, trinity.

The answer to this thesis given by George Stigler and by other critics has been that it is a mistake to suppose that these concentrated groups are always on *different* sides. After all, big business and big labour have *common* interests *vis-a-vis* the consumer. It will be in the self-interest of both groups to operate together to exploit the consumer. In any event, far from this being a countervailing power, or a power that would restore stability and offset the harm done by large conglomerations, it intensifies the harm. Cartel agreements are unstable; and agreements among bilateral or multilateral monopolists are unstable. In any case, the whole Galbraithian argument is factually incorrect. The evidence is that some of the *largest* concentrations of union power are in industries in which the employers have very *little* concentration of power. In the United States, for example, the coal miners' is a major concentrated union, able to gain advantages for its members by acting as a monopolising agent for the industry because the industry itself is so *dispersed*. The coal miners in effect run a cartel on behalf of the employers. Similarly, the teamsters' union, certainly one of the strongest in the United States, did not arise as a countervailing power to some pre-existing corporate monopoly. It arose in part because there was *dispersed* power from which it was able to benefit.

[1]Published under the title *American Capitalism: Concept of Countervailing Power,* Hamish Hamilton, 1952.

[2]*American Economic Review, Papers and Proceedings,* May 1954, pp. 7-14.

Whither the 'new industrial state'?

This theme of countervailing power is one to which Kenneth Galbraith has in recent years paid almost no attention. He has largely dropped it by the wayside because he has discovered a more attractive way to approach the same objective. And that is through his most ambitious book, *The New Industrial State,*[1] in which he seeks to bring up to date Thorstein Veblen's *The Engineers and the Price System,*[2] with a good deal of help from James Burnham's *The Managerial Revolution.*[3]

This book implied largely a rejection of the thesis of countervailing power in favour of the thesis that control of society is in the hands of a technical-managerial class, the 'technostructure'. One of Galbraith's great abilities is his ability to seize upon key words and sell them. He is an advertiser *par excellence!* It has always puzzled me why the commercial advertising industry has not recognised that and taken advantage of his extraordinary quality. 'The affluent society' was one such phrase. 'Countervailing power' was another. Now somehow I would think that if you started out with such a clumsy word as 'technostructure' it would not exactly become a common saying, a household word — yet it seems to have caught on very well indeed! The key theme of *The New Industrial State,* as you all know, is that the economy is dominated by giant concerns in which control is in the hands of the technical-managerial class. These have grown so large that individuals are no longer important as entrepreneurs: stockholders play a purely passive role of approving whatever actions management takes and serve no important entrepreneurial function.

This managerial class, according to Galbraith, has as its chief aim security for itself. And it seems to achieve that security by controlling both those who supply goods and services to the enterprise and those who purchase its product. It seems to control both suppliers and demanders, and it does so, of course, with the aid of government. It establishes an effective coalition with the governmental authorities. And together with government it can secure its own future.

[1] Pelican Books, 1969.

[2] Harbinger Books, 1963; Augustus Kelley, New York, 1970.

[3] Indiana University Press, 1960 (reprinted by Greenwood Press, New York, 1972).

It controls its suppliers by being a monopolistic purchaser, the prime source of demand for their products. It controls the demanders by the use of persuasive advertising. This theme from *The Affluent Society* is one that is central to Galbraith's view throughout this whole series of books. In his view the market plays a very minor role indeed. True, there remain some enterprises such as agriculture, small service trades, and so on, which are essentially competitive enterprises subject to market control and market pressure. But they are a tail that is wagged by the dog of the large corporate giants, which in Galbraith's view typify the modern economy.

This view has also been examined and attacked by many scholars. John Jewkes, in his book on *The Sources of Invention,*[1] examines Galbraith's claim that the day of the small enterpriser is past, that, in Galbraith's words as quoted by Jewkes, 'a benign providence has made the modern industry of a few large firms an almost perfect instrument for inducing technical change'. Jewkes examines this claim and writes at the close of his book:

'Nearly all the systematic evidence has run counter to any such doctrine. Yet, so far as we are aware, Professor Galbraith has said nothing in defence, or in modification, of his views'.[2]

Lack of realism and understanding

The validity of Galbraith's picture of the industrial world was attacked from a very different point of view by Sir Frank McFadzean, who is sitting here in the audience and so can correct me if I misrepresent his critique. Sir Frank attacked Galbraith for a lack of realism, and misunderstanding of how large enterprises are run. He attacked the realism of Galbraith's view from the inside, as it were, and demonstrated, I think rather conclusively in a lecture he gave some 10 years ago,[3] that the notion that somehow or other large enterprises were run by faceless impersonal committees with the ability to control their future was a

---

[1]Written with David Sawers and Richard Stillerman, Macmillan, London, 1959 (2nd Edition 1969).

[2]*Ibid.,* p. 227.

[3]*Galbraith and the Planners,* Strathclyde University Press, 1968.

fairy-tale rather than an accurate description.

Galbraith was similarly attacked by Professor G. C. Allen in an excellent *Paper*[1] published by the Institute of Economic Affairs, on similar grounds, but with rather more attention to the behaviour of aggregates, such as industry as a whole, than to the behaviour of particular enterprises. Finally, some studies have been made by an American economist, Harold Demsetz, formerly at the University of Chicago but currently at the University of California at Los Angeles; he tested three of the Galbraithian hypotheses statistically to see whether the facts coincided with them. Galbraith had emphasised that defence industries were the examples *par excellence* of industries that were capable of controlling their own destinies because they had the government for a client and could effectively control the demand for their products, the prices at which they sold, and the like. Demsetz proceeded to examine the evidence.[2] He examined the market behaviour of the stocks of 13 large defence-oriented industries in the United States. Lo and behold, he found that the real return from investing in those stocks was much more variable from year to year than the average of all other stocks! It may have been necessary at that time to go to the stock market, but one need merely today observe the fate of some of the defence giants in the United States like Lockheed, General Dynamics and the like, to recognise that they are very, very far indeed from being in a position to control their own destiny. And not even very large expenditures on persuasive advertising in foreign countries enables them to do so.

'No evidence'

Professor Demsetz also examined two other hypotheses of Galbraith's. You would find his article[3] extremely interesting because he points out how difficult it is to get testable hypotheses out of the Galbraithian canon. Galbraith speaks in broad general

[1] *Economic Fact and Fantasy: A rejoinder to Galbraith's Reith Lectures,* Occasional Paper 14, IEA, 1967 (Second Edition 1969).

[2] 'Economics in the Industrial State — Discussion', *American Economic Review,* May 1970.

[3] 'Where is the New Industrial State?', *Economic Inquiry* (Journal of the Western Economics Association), March 1974.

terms; he makes assertions about the world at large. But they are very seldom put in a form in which they yield testable hypotheses. In addition to the one about defence industries, Demsetz tested, through multiple correlation of the experience of many enterprises, the Galbraithian theme that technostructure-oriented firms sacrifice profits to accelerate the growth of sales. Galbraith's theme here is that once you get one of these large corporations with the technocrats in the technostructure in command, they have to have certain minimal profits in order to satisfy the stockholders and keep them quiet, but beyond that what they really want to do is to grow. And so, argues Galbraith, they are willing to sacrifice profits for the sake of sales. Demsetz proceeded to assemble data on firms and to classify them as technostructure-oriented by the kind of criteria Galbraith used. He then tried to see whether it was true that there was a trade-off of profits against sales. *He could find no evidence for it whatsoever.*

He also investigated Galbraith's thesis that such firms use the control of prices, of advertising and of government intervention to prevent the disruption of their plans. Again he did this by trying to see whether firms of that type in practice have more stable income and profits than other firms. Again he found no confirmation at all of this Galbraithian claim.

Misinterpretation of economic theory and research

There have been many other criticisms of Galbraith's views, including many by people who are politically very sympathetic to his orientation, such as for example the extremely critical review of *The New Industrial State* by Robert Solow,[1] in which he criticised Galbraith as misinterpreting both economic theory and recent research. The claim that the mangers can neglect the stockholders because enterprises are large has itself been subjected to an enormous amount of study. We all know that the stock market exerts an influence in a very indirect but effective way. And, no matter how large the enterprise, if the managers act in

[1]Professor Robert M. Solow's critique, 'The New Industrial State, or Son of Affluence', appeared in *The Public Interest*, No. 9, 1967. Professor Galbraith's reply, in the same issue, was entitled 'A Review of a Review'. Professor Solow responded with 'A Rejoinder'.

such a way as to earn less than is feasible with those resources, this has an effect on the price of the stock. If the stock price is driven down it provides somebody with an incentive to buy up the stock, engage in take-over activity, and in this way kick out the current management. And there have been enough cases of this occurring for every manager in every major enterprise to recognise where his own self-interest lies.

It is very interesting indeed that the enterprises which come closest, in my opinion, to conforming to Galbraith's picture of the modern giants are some of the *nationalised* industries, because there indeed there is no effective stock market to enforce on the managers the promotion of the interests of the enterprise.

The main purpose of going over this examination of the evidence is that, so far as I know, apart from Galbraith's own assertion, *there has been no successful defence of this view of the world.* That does not mean there are no defenders of the view. There are many. There are many who accept it. But I know of no scientific studies which have validated that view of the world as meaningful and accurate in the sense that it yields predictions about the behaviour of enterprises, of industry, or of the economy as a whole that can be checked, tested against evidence, and found to hold.

III
GALBRAITH — SCIENTIST OR MISSIONARY?

And that brings me back to the puzzle I started with. How can so intelligent, thoughtful and independent a mind as Kenneth Galbraith's hold such an apparently indefensible view of reality? The basis for an answer, I think, is to be found by re-examining Galbraith's purpose and approach. Instead of regarding him as a scientist seeking explanations, I think we shall get more understanding if we look at him as a missionary seeking converts. We must therefore examine not his evidence, not his hypotheses, but his values and his philosophy, his ideology. If we do so I think we shall see that his view of the world derives from his ideological view, and not the other way round.

Galbraith a Tory Radical?

Galbraith has always seemed to me a 20th-century version of the early 19th-century Tory Radicals of Great Britain. Some of you will have read a book by Cecil Driver called *Tory Radical: The Life of Richard Oastler.*[1] At any rate, there was a group of Tories in the early 19th century called Tory Radicals, whose position was, as I see it, very similar to Galbraith's position today. They believed in an aristocracy, as he does. They knew they were members of that aristocracy, as he does. They had membership in it by virtue of birth; he has membership in it by virtue of other qualities. They believed that the aristocracy had an obligation to the masses and that they were the only disinterested group in the community that could serve the masses, because their position came to them naturally, without effort necessarily on their part, and this provided them with an obligation at the same time that it in large measure assured their disinterestedness. They believed, however, that they should not — and Galbraith believes that he should not — use force to impose their views on the masses. Their approach was fully paternalistic: they were in a position of a father to children, whose children would naturally recognise the superiority of the father and that his values were superior to theirs. And so the Tory Radicals expected, and thought it appropriate, that the masses would accept the dominion of the aristocrats over their values and beliefs, because the aristocrats were seeking their welfare. I believe that Galbraith's view is essentially the same. He is not in favour of any kind of imposition on the masses of the values he stands for. He knows that his values are superior to those of the masses, and he thinks that if the masses are properly instructed by enough of his books, they will come themselves to that view and will ask him and his fellow intellectuals to take charge.

He has thus always reminded me of the Tory Radicals, but Shirley and William Letwin[2] and others have persuaded me that there is also a strong admixture of John Stuart Mill's philosophical radicalism. I can demonstrate that element most quickly and

[1]Octagon, New York, 1946 (reprinted 1970).

[2][William Letwin is professor of Political Science at the London School of Economics. His wife, Shirley Robin Letwin, has taught, *inter alia,* at the LSE and is the author of *The Pursuit of Certainty,* Cambridge University Press, 1965, and other words. — ED.]

effectively by reading a few quotations from Maurice Cowling's book on *Mill and Liberalism.*[1] You will see that each of these quotations, which Maurice Cowling regards as applicable to John Stuart Mill, is every bit as applicable to Galbraith.

First:

'. . . "the higher minds" should set the tone of the society in which they live; and hence . . . *their* sort of education in general culture must be propagated as extensively as possible'. (p. 37)

Second:

'. . . Mill's fundamental principles have neither proof nor philosophical authority, but are commitments to action, the outcome of assertions to claim knowledge of the nature of the world and the direction men's duty ought to take within it: . . . it is difficult to avoid feeling that much of what we will characterise as his *arrogance* is connected with want of clarity at this point.' (p. 77)

Note that 'want of clarity' is about whether his assertions have scientific authority.

There is no-one who does not apply the word 'arrogant' to Galbraith, and with justice. It applies precisely for the reason that Cowling refers to it in Mill: because Galbraith treats his assertions as if they have scientific authority, as if they have been demonstrated, when they have not been at all. His principles, as Cowling says about Mill's, are commitments to action.

Third:

'Mill was one of the most censorious of 19th-century moralists. At every turn, denigration of existing society is offered with inquisitorial certainty . . .'. (p. 143)

Finally:

'If a writer believes a doctrine he is promulgating, and feels an obligation to it, he is unlikely to reveal its limitations'. (p. 147)

Reconciling lack of evidence with dogmatic conviction

That brings me back to my main theme: the reconciliation

[1]Cambridge University Press, 1963.

of the factual inadequacy of the Galbraithian view and the dogmatic confidence with which he asserts it. I want to show how you can link the position he takes about the world with his ideological and philosophical view.

First, Galbraith's Tory Radical position implies that the values of the masses are inferior to those of the intellectual aristocracy, and that, of course, is the theme that runs throughout his analysis. But, moreover, if the values of the masses are created by self-interested advocates in industry, then they have no claim to be considered as valid, or to be respected. Thus, in order for Galbraith to strengthen his emphasis on the right of the aristocracy to shape the values of the masses, it is extremely convenient to be able to treat those values as having no validity but simply as the creation of self-interested advocates.

This has further implications. It is possible for values to be altered by advertising, Mill's 'higher minds' can affect them too. After all, if these commercial advertisers can shape man's life, there is meaning to having a society in which the higher minds can shape man's wants and values. And you can have some success from this Tory radical political programme of the leading aristocrats, so there is point to having them in power.

Moreover, if you have rule by a free market, if a free market really ruled in response to valid consumer wants, that would provide an alternative to rule by higher minds. It would also render such rule difficult or impossible to achieve. Many reformers — Galbraith is not alone in this — have as their basic objection to a free market that it frustrates them in achieving their reforms, because it enables people to have what they want, not what the reformers want. Hence every reformer has a strong tendency to be adverse to a free market. Galbraith in particular must regard it as trivial or non-existent, or else his whole ideological case, both its justification and its possibility, collapses.

If the free market is not the ruler, who are the rulers? Not, according to Galbraith, entrepreneurs serving the market, but technocrats, who have no moral authority. Besides, they are not disinterested. These technocrats are self-selected, they make their own jobs, they appoint one another. What right do they have to decide people's tastes, how the resources of a community should be used? If you had Adam Smith entrepreneurs running the society in response to the demands of the public, that would have some moral authority. But the technocrats have no moral authority: they are running it in their own interest.

I believe that this is a very important feature in the Galbraithian view. It serves both to justify his emphasis on rule by the intellectual class and also to enhance its appeal to the public at large. We all want somebody to blame things on. Nothing that happens that is bad is our fault; it's other people who do it to us. And all the better if those other people are faceless bureaucrats in the private sector whom we did not elect, we did not choose. They just somehow got there.

Incidentally if the technocracy rules, if the technocracy fixed prices and wages for its own convenience, then government officials can do so also. Howver, as I mentioned earlier, Galbraith's attitude towards price and wage control is not really central to his position. You can subtract it and leave his position unaltered. It is really peripheral to it; it arises out of the sheer accident that he happened to spend part of World War II as a price controller.

This interpretation of Galbraith's view of the world seems to me to make it all of one piece and explains his subbornness in adhering to it. The characteristics he attributes to the world are essential to upholding his values, his ideological and his political position. But it also explains the grounds on which other people object to it, including myself. The philosophical radicals, like the socialists, attacked the aristocracy. In this they were quite a bit different from Galbraith. On the other hand, they were similar to Galbraith in that insofar as there were to be leaders they wanted them to be a meritocracy rather than an aristocracy. And in this respect Galbraith joins them.

Meritocracy or aristocracy — the lesser evil

I must say I object to being ruled either by the natural-born aristocracy or by a meritocracy but, if I have to be ruled by either it seems to me that aristocracy of birth is much the lesser evil if only because those born to be aristocrats are less likely to be arrogant. They know it is an accident. This was of course the endearing feature of the Tory Radicals, that they recognised they were accidentally in the position of leadership. This is what, in their view, gave them their obligations to the rest of the community, their *noblesse oblige*. But a meritocracy, people who know that they are *abler* than their fellows, and are therefore in a position to rule? Heaven forbid!

More fundamentally, of course, I object to the view that any aristocracy should rule. I believe it is of the utmost arrogance for any of us to suppose that we have the right to decide what is the better and the worse value for others by any means other than persuasion. We may of course have strong views of our own: we may believe very strongly that poetry is better than pushpin, or the reverse. But for those of us who believe in the dignity of the individual human being, in the pre-eminence of freedom among human beings as the objective of social organisation: we must say that the only way in which we have any right to try to affect the values of others is by persuasion. And that, I may say, includes commercial advertising, which I view as a form of free speech and which ought to be just as much subject as other forms of discourse to the First Amendment of the United States Consttution prohibiting governmental measures against free speech. (The US Supreme Court, I am delighted to say, has recently so ruled.)

Galbraith v. Adam Smith

These are, I believe, the fundamental grounds on which the battle is drawn. Throughout all history there have been the superiors who have believed that they have the right to rule the inferiors. And the only method of social and economic organisation that has ever been developed which avoids that result is the method which Adam Smith espoused in his *Wealth of Nations:* voluntary co-operation among individuals in which each man is free to use his own capacities and resources as he wills in accordance with his own values so long as he does not interfere with the right of others to do likewise. That is a view of the world which is profoundly opposed by the Galbraithian view of the world.

Galbraith would not oppose the Adam Smith view explicitly

as undesirable; he never does that. He would agree with every word I have just said. But if he were here he would say:

'Ah, but you're a visionary. That's unrealistic. That isn't the way the world really is. Technical development and technical growth have made it essential that we have these large corporations and these large governments and these large organisations. And therefore your picture is a dream, a Utopia that is incapable of achievement.'

This is a claim which I believe the various critics of Galbraith have shown to be unfounded. These large enterprises are in practice not large relative to the market as a whole, not any larger than they were a hundred years ago. Large governments are not produced, and have not been produced, by technical necessities making things occur on a larger scale. There is no technical necessity arising out of technological development that requires an expansion of welfare programmes, of rent controls, of government housing, of public health. Not one of these reflects technological pressure.

They reflect rather an erroneous approach of trying to use *political* methods to achieve good objectives. The growth of government reflects rather the invisible hand in politics which works in the opposite direction from the invisible hand in economics.

In *economics* those people who attempt to pursue only their own self-interest are led by an invisible hand to promote the *public* interest.

In the *political* sphere individuals like Galbraith who attempt to pursue the public interest as they view it are led by an invisible hand to further *private* interests which it is no part of their intention to promote.

PART II
THE ROAD TO ECONOMIC FREEDOM:
THE STEPS FROM HERE TO THERE

Before we start on the discussion I cannot resist informing some of you, and Arthur Seldon[1] in particular, that there are some respects in which American trade unions are worse than British trade unions. I have just discovered one this afternoon, in taping a brief comment for the BBC. In the United States if a gentleman like Terence Kelly[2] came around to interview me with a cassette tape recorder and one side of the cassette tape ran out and he had to turn it over, that cassette would be wiped out when he got back to the office because it is the function of a technician, not of a reporter, to turn the cassette over. And so he has to be sure that he can record everything on one side of the cassette! But here in Britain I saw Terence here — and this is a tape recorder rather than a cassette recorder — actually put in a new tape! Now that surely is a job for a technician! Now why is that? Because the trade unions don't think there's enough fat in the BBC to go after? What the reason is, I don't know, but at any rate you'll be glad to know that you've got some advantages.

We need to divide the major question 'from here to there' into two very different issues. One has to do with the problem of how you get out of the kind of situation in which Britain now is, with something like 60 per cent of the national income being spent by government, and with an inflation which has gone up and down for years. How you turn that situation around and get the basic economic structure of the economy into a healthy situation is one class of problem. There is a second and very different class of problem: how do you unwind the various social welfare or industrial intervention measures that your government undertakes? The first is a problem of general financial policy and the second of detailed social and economic policy.

[1] [A reference to a deviation from the monetarist view that trade unions have no direct role in generating inflation. The deviating view is that unions in strong bargaining positions can in Britain induce government to inflate in order to stimulate demand and so avoid the unemployment that would follow monopoly labour costs that cannot be passed on in higher prices. The process is not 'cost-push', but 'politicial-push'; the mechanism or instrument of inflation remains the money supply, mismanaged by government monopoly. — ED.]

[2] [The BBC interviewer; he is the producer of the BBC radio programme 'Dateline'. — ED.]

I
THE IMMEDIATE FINANCIAL TASK

The first of these is in some ways the immediate problem that a country like Britain is faced with. Suppose you had the will, which you haven't, how should you go about trying to get the economy on to a healthy basis?

Gradualism

Now in this particular issue I believe that one major question is gradualism *versus* shock treatment. That is a question to which the same answer cannot be given under all circumstances. If you are in the situation of the United States today, with an inflation rate running at about 6 per cent a year, total governmental spending at about 40 per cent of the national income — in which we have been getting worse but are at a much less advanced state of the disease than you are — I am all in favour of a very gradual return to a non-inflationary position. I would not be in favour of trying to get a zero rate of inflation next year because there are all sorts of contracts people have entered into, including borrowing and lending contracts at rates of interest that implicitly allow for a considerable measure of inflation. There are employment contracts, building contracts, and so on, and it would be very disturbing to the arrangements voluntarily reached amongst individuals if you were overnight to go from, say, 6 per cent to zero. I think in the United States it would be desirable to go to zero over a period of four or five years, by cutting down the rate of inflation by about 1 per cent per year. Personally I would like to see that policy announced in advance so that people could adjust themselves to it. And I would call that a relatively gradual approach to a state of financial equilibrium.

Shock Treatment

On the other hand, to take the extreme opposite case: a year ago I was in Chile which was faced with the problem of an inflation of 20 per cent a *month*. Now that is a different story altogether. To talk about that country trying to reduce its inflation rate at the rate of 1 per cent a year is silly. A country in that position has very few long-term contracts. One of the major effects of such a rapid rate of inflation is that people do not engage in long-term contracts which are contingent upon what the rate of inflation is going to be. Liquid resources are very small. Total money supply in Chile at that time amounted to three days' payment. It's a hand-to-mouth situation of the most extreme kind, because of course if prices are going up at 20 per cent a month you are going to make arrangements to keep to a very minimum the amount of cash or non-interest-earning assets you hold. And under those circumstances it seemed to me, as I argued then, as I would now, that the only sensible thing to do is a shock treatment, in which you make a very sharp move. You get the figure right away and try to bring the inflation rate down to your long-term objective in a very short period.

These are not only hypothetical questions. We have a good deal of historical experience. There are two very important episodes in recent decades which illustrate how effective a shock treatment of that kind can be. One is the German Erhard episode in 1948, when Erhard terminated all wage and price controls over one weekend. He did it on a Sunday because the American, British and French occupation offices were closed and they would not be able to countermand his orders! A very similar situation occurred in Japan about the same time, in response to a mission from the United States headed by a banker from Detroit by the name of Dodge. The Japanese again used essentially shock treatment of a monetary reform, substituting a new money under new circumstances, cutting government spending sharply, getting the government's budget into a more tolerable position. In both cases you had very favourable results. Of course they were unfavourable aspects of the immediate shock, but they lasted only a short period, because you did not have long-term contracts built into the system that are the major source of difficulty in unwinding a high inflation.

Chile and Britain

In Chile they engaged in a shock treatment but only went halfway. They cut the growth of the money supply from something over 20 per cent a *month* to something over 10 per cent a month and brought the inflation rate down from 20 per cent a month to 10 per cent a month. I was very interested in the Chilean case because certain of the fundamental parameters were almost identical with those of the British case. The government deficit in Chile, which was being financed by printing money, was about 10 per cent of the national income. At that time the British government deficit, or borrowing requirement, was also roughly 10 per cent of the national income.

The reason why you are able to get away with so much lower an inflation rate of 20 per cent a *year* instead of 20 per cent a *month* is, first, that you are in a position to borrow half of that from overseas. Chile was not. Secondly, you did not have the long background of inflation as a result of which the Chileans had reduced their money holding to such small totals as three days' spending. In the United Kingdom you had a much larger total of liquid assets, so that inflation was a very much more productive tax in the United Kingdom than in Chile. To finance a budget deficit equal to 5 per cent of the national income by printing money thus required an inflation tax of only 20 or 25 per cent a year, and not 20 per cent a month as in Chile. But if Britain were to continue along these lines, those advantages would disappear, and you would be unable to borrow abroad. The tax would become progressively a less productive source of revenue, and to finance similar deficits you would have to engage in ever higher levels of inflation.

Modified shock treatment for Britain

The British case is not the American case and it is not the Chilean, German or Japanese cases — it is in between. And yet I think it is far enough along the way towards the German, Japanese or Chilean cases to make Britain a good candidate for a shock treatment, and not for a very gradualistic approach to cutting inflation at a slow rate over a long period. By shock treatment again I do not mean it would be feasible for you to bring the rate of inflation down to zero next month. But I see no reason why you should not try to establish guidelines and policies which would bring you into a roughly zero inflation within something like three to five years.

The instruments

What is required in order to do that? What do I mean by a shock treatment? The shock treatment can work in the British case if, and only if, it enables Britain to cut down the amount of money it has to create to finance its obligations. How can it do that?

Number one, and most importantly, you must cut government spending. I have no doubt that the absolute *sine qua non* of a non-inflationary policy in Britain is a cut. I do *not* mean a cut in the prospective *increase;* I mean a real cut in government spending and a cut that is substantial. That is the first requisite. Look at your figures now. You are spending something like 60 per cent of the national income through the government. Your explicit taxes are raising at most something like 50 per cent of the national income, and then only with systems of taxes which have severe disincentive effects on working, saving, and investing. The first step has to be to eliminate the need to finance that 10 per cent. That means a very minimum objective is to cut government spending from 60 down to 50 per cent of national income — something like that — within three years.

You could go further than that. The cut in government spending by a sixth is not a major magnitude. It would not reduce efficiency. There is little doubt that if you were to go through every government bureau in the United Kingdom and fire every sixth man, the productivity of the other five would go up rather than down. Your own experience of a three-day week in industry in February 1974 was very impressive evidence from that point of view. But the *political* difficulty is of course very severe, because the immediate initial effect of such cutting looks as if it is adding to unemployment. It is really not adding to unemployment. Rather it is rendering people available for *productive* employment instead of *unproductive* employment. Most of those people would be absorbed in a fairly brief period.

In any event, the only question that arises is: How can you cut government spending by that much? I have come to a very simple conclusion. There is only one way to do it. It is *not* by looking for places where money is wasted, *not* by seeking the worst workplaces, but *across the board.* You have to do it by saying:

every department, every office is going to have a statutory obligation to make cuts year by year. It seems to me the only way to cut that is feasible is to say that this year every office, every department, is to be cut by 10 per cent; next year it is to be cut by another 10 per cent; and the year after that by another 10 per cent. And only then do you arrange the cuts as you will within departments. Only then can you consider the special case and have each department fight with every other department for a change in that total allocation. But once you start along the lines 'We're going to find waste', you will find that it is universal and then you open the door to the special interest behind each particular activity to bring their full pressure to bear; and you are then back in the whole story of special interest politics.

The public at large, I think, is much more likely to support a policy — indeed it has begun to support a policy — that says 'We are going to cut government spending from 60 per cent of the national income to 50 per cent in the next two or three years, and we are going to do it across the board'. If you start arguing with the public at large, by saying, 'We can get rid of a little bit of this department' or 'There's a wasteful activity here', it will be hopeless to get backing for it. That seems to me, from an economic point of view, to be the sensible way to go about your cuts in government spending.

Tax system reform by shock treatment

The second requisite of course is to reorganise the tax structure. Here again I think you really need a shock treatment and not a gradual move in one direction or another. There is nobody in your country or mine who does not recognise that our present tax system is a mess. It does not in practice achieve any of the objectives claimed for it. It taxes people who are in the same position differently, depending on the source of their income and on the accident of whether they can escape the tax.

One of the striking things that always seems a paradox to people from overseas who come to visit Britain is that they are puzzled as to why there are so many Rolls-Royces in a country on the verge of destruction, in which productivity has been going downhill, in which you have had great inefficiency, and in which the government has been dedicated these many years to egalitarianism. How come all these Rolls-Royces? And then you see the prices charged for second-hand Rolls-Royces. How can these people afford to pay £10,000, £20,000 for Rolls-Royces? The answer is very simple, as you know better than anybody else. It is the *cheapest* way in the world for anybody who has wealth to try to conserve it and also to buy transportation. If the alternative to investing that wealth in a Rolls-Royce is to invest it in income-yielding securities, most of the income is going to go to the tax collector, whereas it does not cost anything to have a Rolls-Royce. A man invests, say £30,000 in a Rolls-Royce. If he invested it in income-earning securities, earning, say, 15 per cent, he would get a gross yield of £4,500 a year. If he's in the 98 per cent tax bracket he has only £90 a year left after tax to spend. So it costs him only £90 a year to have his Rolls-Royce all year! It's the cheapest form of transportation he can possibly buy! In addition, he has the advantage of an asset that will conserve some of its capital value. If he put it in government bonds, then every year it is going to be worth less, even aside from the amount that the government takes from him in taxes. And so your tax system discourages saving and investment. *It encourages wasteful, 'conspicuous' consumption.*

Again, if I ask what it costs an employer to employ a man, on the one hand, and what is the net yield to a man from being employed, on the other, I find both in your country and mine the tax system has introduced a very large wedge. I do not understand why people are puzzled by the phenomenon of simultaneous higher unemployment benefit and lower employment. Economic principles work: if you increase the demand for anything, the supply will grow to meet it. In your country and mine we have made it ever more attractive to be unemployed. *We have increased the demand for unemployment,* and the supply of unemployed has risen to meet that demand. On the other hand, we have imposed a heavy tax on employing anyone. So the result is that we have made employers unwilling to employ people. The wedge between the cost to the employer and the net return to the employee has become bigger and bigger.

Indexation and lower tax rates

I know what I would say in the United States, but I do not know enough of the British tax system to assess how I would go about reconstructing it in Britain. But I do know what the essential features are: first, indexation of the tax system so as to eliminate the tendency for inflation to push people up into ever-higher brackets and to eliminate the temptation for governments to use inflation as a way of financing their business. Secondly, a reduction in the special allowances and a sharp reduction along with that in the marginal rate of tax. You can raise the present revenue at vastly *lower* taxes if you apply the tax rates to the *whole* of the income, however earned and received, with no tax-free allowances. In the United States we have tax rates that go from 14 per cent at the bottom to 70 per cent at the top. You have rates which go up much higher than that. But if you eliminated the special deductions, exemptions and so-called loopholes from the income tax in the United States, you could raise the same revenue with the same personal exemptions with, I think, a flat rate of around 16 per cent. And in practice you would raise a lot more than that.

In a column I wrote a year or so ago[1] I demonstrated pretty conclusively, I think, that the United States government would get more revenue than it now gets from the personal income tax if it made no change in the law except to replace all tax rates above 25 per cent by 25 per cent. That change would yield *more* revenue because it would make it unprofitable for people to resort to the tax gimmicks and loopholes[2] they now use. *They would report more revenue.* The taxpayer would be better off and the Exchequer would be better off. One of the great mistakes people make in taxation policy is to treat the tax receipts of the government as if they corresponded to the cost of the taxes to the taxpayer. They do not. Because of the existence of the tax system, taxpayers are led to do all sorts of things (in the form of tax avoidance or evasion, including not working or engaging in occupations different from those they would engage in if taxes were

[1] *Newsweek,* 12 April, 1976.

[2] [The effects of high tax rates in 'gimmicks and loopholes', etc., are discussed by Dr. Barry Bracewell-Milnes in a Hobart Paper to be published in 1977. — ED.]

lower) that are very costly to them but which yield no revenue to the government. It is this difference between the total cost to the taxpayer and the total receipts to the government that offers the opportunity for reductions that will benefit both the revenue and the taxpayer. This is the second shock treatment you badly need in the sense of a very substantial modification and change in the tax system.

I have only one other thing to say on how you get back to a non-inflationary state. I think it is right to put emphasis on how you hold down the quantity of money, but I think it is wrong to suppose that it is some kind of simple cure that can be introduced without affecting anything else. The real problem is to adjust the budget and government expenditures in such a way that it is feasible to hold down the rate of growth of the quantity of money.

II
UNWINDING GOVERNMENT

Now let us suppose by some miracle you really had a political regime that was committed to moving away from the kind of welfare state, nationalised apparatus that Britain has, and that the US has been increasingly moving towards, and wanted to get to a largely free enterprise state in which people had a good deal more leeway about how they handled their own resources than they have now. What general principles can you think of that are relevant in proceeding from here to there?

Denationalisation by auctioning or giving away

Once again in some cases it is appropriate to get rid of it all at once. Most of these cases have to do with nationalisation of economic activities. I do not see any sense in saying 'We are going to "privatise" the steel industry piece meal' or 'We are going to sell off to the public 1 per cent of the steel industry each year'. The obvious thing to do with the steel industry, the railroads, and all those industries currently governmentally operated is to get rid of them by auctioning then off. Here there are various devices. At the moment it would be very hard to auction off the steel industry, because a Tory government did it once and then a Labour government renationalised it and anybody who buys it again would now be very uncertain that he would be able to retain ownership. One suggestion a number of people have made which I think makes a great deal of sense would be, not to auction it off, but to give it away, by giving every citizen in the country a share in it.

After all, the supposed argument is that the people of Great Britain own the steel industry; it is the property of all the citizens. Well, then, why not give each citizen his piece? Now you may say this raises some questions of feasibility. You might say 55 million shares are a lot of shares — in order to have a market in them you would have to re-introduce the farthing to enable people to buy and sell them. That's true.

A mutual fund

But it seems to me you could go at it in a very different way. You have not only the steel industry, but electricity, the BBC, railroads, road transport, etc. Suppose you constructed a mutual fund to which you assigned the shares in all these enterprises and then gave every one of the 55 million citizens of the United Kingdom a share in it. Now you are talking about magnitudes that are perfectly feasible.

I do not think individuals would regard a share in such a fund as derisory. And I do not see why that really is not the kind of approach you want to adopt because it meets every socialist value. These enterprises belong to the people; so we are going to give them to the people. This method has a big advantage. If you tried to auction these industries off individually, the *government* would get the revenue and it would waste it. But if you give it to the *people,* and you allow a market to be established, you would see in a very short period that this would unsnarl itself. In the first place, individuals would start to buy and sell the mutual shares they were given. In the second place, the mutual enterprise, would see a market starting to be established in its stock. Perhaps you would need three or four mutuals. I am not going into details; I am trying to get at the principles. The fundamental principle is to do it in a way which gives the public at large a strong incentive to have it done, and not in a way which is simply another channel for the government to acquire revenue, as for example the UK government did in selling off the steel industry in the first place and then renationalising it. I think that kind of unwinding ought to be done all at once.

Towards profitability

But what if most of these industries now make a loss? They would not, once they were liberated from government control. You accomplish two purposes at once: you reduce the governmental deficit at the same time as you provide for a more efficient private economy. It may be reasonable, in 'privatising' them — in giving them to the mutual fund — for Parliament to provide a guarantee of a year or two of subsidy to enable them to get on their feet.

Let us leave aside the political issue and examine the economic issue. Suppose I say I want to auction off the steel industry. It may be that its market price as now nationalised is negative. Therefore the auction procedure might be for the government to say:'Who will take the steel industry off our hands for the least subsidy?' And similarly with the mutual fund. But from a political point of view it seems to me far more preferable to distribute it amongst the public at large than to try to do it by paying somebody to take it off your hands. And if the trade unions object, then give the nationalised industries to the unions.

III
REDUCTION OF GOVERNMENT BY GRADUALISM

Now I want to go on to the other class of policies where you need to proceed more gradually. These are the classic cases in which you have a government that has put individuals in a position where they are dependent on government bounty and in which you cannot really throw them out overnight. As a result of the welfare state measures that your country and my country have undertaken, millions of people today are dependent on the bounty of the state for their livelihood, and you cannot simply say we are going to cut that off overnight and throw them out on the street. The question here is, then, different. How do you set up arrangements which will simultaneously enable you to wind down those programmes but at the same time do not create great difficulties for settled expectations?

Vouchers or cash

Here I think the one principle which can be applied is that in general you can do so by trying to substitute vouchers or cash payments for services in kind or vouchers for particular groups in place of across-the-board payments and subsidies to everybody.

The voucher scheme has received perhaps most attention in education. Certainly it is, in my opinion, about the only feasible way to go from the government-dominated educational system we now have to the kind under which you have a free, competitive private-market educational system. That would be desirable. The virtues of the voucher system are in my opinion two-fold. One is that it introduces choice and enables competition to come into effect. That is the virtue that has been most discussed. But for the moment I want to discuss another virtue of a very different kind.

This is the possibility of winding things down, of reducing the fraction of the total costs borne by the government and thereby returning activities to the private sector. Ask anybody the abstract question: Is the case for governmental provision of education stronger in a poor society or in an affluent society? Or, is it more appropriate to expect parents to pay for the schooling of their children in a poor country or in a rich country? Almost everybody will answer: 'Obviously in a rich country it is more appropriate for parents to pay and there is more of a case for governmental provision in a poor country'. And yet *historically the relationship has been the other way round.*

In your country and my country, as we have become richer, the fraction of total educational expenditure that is borne by the state has gone *up*. Why? I believe the major reason is that governments have financed education through running educational *institutions*. They have set up schools and run them and therefore there has been no way in which private individuals could spend private money in a marginal way. As societies became more affluent people at large wanted to spend more on education but, given that government was providing the education, that led to more *government* provision.

Now one of the great virtues of a voucher system is that it makes it possilbe to move in the other direction. If you have a voucher of a fixed dollar or pound value, as the society gets richer people are encouraged to add to it, to use private provision in a marginal way to improve the kind of education and schooling their children get. You can think of the fraction of total governmental education expenditure declining over time so long as you can hold back the political pressures to raise the value of the vouchers. The political pressure then would not have only one place to go; it could at least be diverted by the opportunity to supplement state provision. Perhaps it would not in fact be diverted, but if you have a people committed to getting back to a free society it seems to me that is one of the great virtues of using vouchers.

Reverse income tax

The same thing goes for housing vouchers or medical vouchers. And of course it goes in a far more fundamental sense for eliminating the specific kinds of vouchers and getting a general voucher in the form of a reverse income tax. Now again, one of the virtues of a reverse income tax — (I once labelled it as a 'negative income tax' but the British use 'reverse income tax'. I must say I think negative income tax is more accurate because a negative tax is a subsidy but a reverse tax is — I don't know what a reverse tax is. Anyway, call it what you will.)[1] — its great virtue is that you do not have a system under which you provide medical care by special provision *in kind,* or provide housing and schooling by special services, and so on. In the first place you need a bureaucracy to administer each of these services and this establishes a very, very strong pressure for their maintenance and extension. I think it is true that the greatest forces in your country and in mine which have been promoting an extension of governmental welfare measures have not been the demand from the public at large, or the pressure of well-meaning reformers, but the internal pressure to extend the civil service to administer it.

[1][The term 'reverse income tax' was coined in IEA writings: *Policy for Poverty,* Research Monograph 20, 1970; *Choice in Welfare, 1970,* 1971; and others. The reason was simply that, if a tax was a payment to the fisc, a tax in reverse was a payment from the fisc. — ED.]

I do not know how many people in Britain have read Pat Moynihan's book on the family assistance plan in the United States,[1] on the problems that arose when Mr. Nixon at one stage proposed what was essentially a negative income tax. The theme of Moynihan's book is that that proposal was largely defeated by the welfare bureaucracy. They were the ones who really stirred up the trouble and defeated the proposal.[2] Look at it the other way: if you can put through a negative income tax as a *substitute* for, not an *addition* to, all the special piecemeal programmes, it has the great virtue that it will enable you to reduce the bureacracy and reduce this pressure. And it also offers some hope that over a period you can gradually reduce the extent to which the government provides, e.g. schooling, as opposed to private provision.

The transition: special cases

One final point on the problem of the transition: in the United States we have tried to work in some detail on some of the special cases — social security, schooling, housing and so on. I cannot really do that for Britain but I think there are two fundamental principles: first, use the market mechanisms as much as you can in turning back the special provisions in kind; second, introduce gradualism of a type which can be made self-destructive.

[1]Daniel P. Moynihan, *The Politics of a Guaranteed Income,* Random House, New York, 1973.

[2][The proposal for an education voucher in the UK, and the moves to an experiment by Kent County Council, are being opposed mainly by the educational bureaucracy in the National Union of Teachers and elsewhere, or rather by the spokesmen for teachers. The voucher idea also met resistance in the Layfield Committee *(Local Government Finance: Report of the Committee of Enquiry,* Cmnd. 6453, HMSO, 1976): Ralph Harris and Arthur Seldon, *Pricing or Taxing?: Evidence to the Layfield Committee and a Critique of its Report,* Hobart Paper 71, IEA, 1976. — ED.]

Chapter 5
Inflation and Unemployment:
The New Dimension of Politics*

When the Bank of Sweden established the prize for Economic Science in memory of Alfred Nobel (1968), there doubtless was — as there doubtless still remains — widespread scepticism among both scientists and the broader public about the appropriateness of treating economics as parallel to physics, chemistry, and medicine. These are regarded as 'exact sciences' in which objective, cumulative, definitive knowledge is possible. Economics, and its fellow social sciences, are regarded more nearly as branches of philosophy than of science properly defined, enmeshed with values at the outset because they deal with human behaviour. Do not the social sciences, in which scholars are analysing the behaviour of themselves and their fellow men, who are in turn observing and reacting to what the scholars say, require fundamentally different methods of investigation than the physical and biological sciences? Should they not be judged by different criteria?

I
SOCIAL AND NATURAL SCIENCES

I have never myself accepted this view. I believe that it reflects a misunderstanding not so much of the character and possibilities of social science as of the character and possibilities of natural science. In both, there is no 'certain' substantive knowledge; only tentative hypotheses that can never be 'proved', but can only fail to be rejected, hypotheses in which we may have more or less confidence, depending on such features as the breadth of experience they encompass relative to their own complexity and relative to alternative hypotheses, and the number of occasions on which they have escaped possible rejection. In both social and natural sciences, the body of positive knowledge grows by the

*Nobel Lecture 1976

©The Nobel Foundation 1977

failure of a tentative hypothesis to predict phenomena the hypothesis professes to explain; by the patching up of that hypothesis until someone suggests a new hypothesis that more elegantly or simply embodies the troublesome phenomena, and so on *ad infinitum*. In both, experiment is sometimes possible, sometimes not (witness meteorology). In both, no experiment is ever completely controlled, and experience often offers evidence that is the equivalent of controlled experiment. In both, there is no way to have a self-contained closed system or to avoid interaction between the observer and the observed. The Gödel theorem in mathematics, the Heisenberg uncertainty principle in physics, the self-fulfilling or self-defeating prophecy in the social sciences all exemplify these limitations.

Of course, the different sciences deal with different subject matter, have different bodies of evidence to draw on (for example, introspection is a more important source of evidence for social than for natural sciences), find different techniques of analysis most useful, and have achieved differential success in predicting the phenomena they are studying. But such differences are as great among, say, physics, biology, medicine, and meteorology as between any of them and economics.

Even the difficult problem of separating value-judgements from scientific judgements is not unique to the social sciences. I well recall a dinner at a Cambridge University college when I was sitting between a fellow economist and R. A. Fisher, the great mathematical statistician and geneticist. My fellow economist told me about a student he had been tutoring on labour economics, who, in connection with an analysis of the effect of trade unions, remarked, 'Well surely, Mr. X (another economist of a different political persuasion) would not agree with that'. My colleague regarded this experience as a terrible indictment of economics because it illustrated the impossibility of a value-free positive economic science. I turned to Sir Ronald and asked whether such an experience was indeed unique to social science. His answer was an impassioned 'no', and he proceeded to tell one story after another about how accurately he could infer views in genetics from political views.

One of my great teachers, Wesley C. Mitchell, impressed on

me the basic reason why scholars have every incentive to pursue a value-free science, whatever their values and however strongly they may wish to spread and promote them. In order to recommend a course of action to achieve an objective, we must first know whether that course of action will in fact promote the objective. Positive scientific knowledge that enables us to predict the consequences of a possible course of action is clearly a prerequisite for the normative judgement whether that course of action is desirable. The Road to Hell is paved with good intentions, precisely because of the neglect of this rather obvious point.

This point is particularly important in economics. Many countries around the world are today experiencing socially destructive inflation, abnormally high unemployment, misuse of economic resources, and in some cases, the suppression of human freedom not because evil men deliberately sought to achieve these results, nor because of differences in values among their citizens, but because of erroneous judgements about the consequences of government measures: errors that at least in principle are capable of being corrected by the progress of positive economic science.

Rather than pursue these ideas in the abstract [I have discussed the methodological issues more fully in (1)], I shall illustrate the positive scientific character of economics by discussing a particular economic issue that has been a major concern of the economics profession throughout the post-war period; namely, the relation between inflation and unemployment. This issue is an admirable illustration because it has been a controversial political issue throughout the period, yet the drastic change that has occurred in accepted professional views was produced primarily by the scientific response to experience that contradicted a tentatively accepted hypothesis — precisely the classical process for the revision of a scientific hypothesis.

I cannot give here an exhaustive survey of the work that has been done on this issue or of the evidence that has led to the revision of the hypothesis. I shall be able only to skim the surface in the hope of conveying the flavour of that work and that evidence and of indicating the major items requiring further investigation.

Professional controversy about the relation between inflation and unemployment has been intertwined with controversy about the relative role of monetary, fiscal, and other factors in influencing aggregate demand. One issue deals with how a change in aggregate nominal demand, however produced, works itself out through changes in employment and price levels; the other, with the factors accounting for the changes in aggregate nominal demand.

The two issues are closely related. The effects of a change in aggregate nominal demand on employment and price levels may not be independent of the source of the change, and conversely, the effect of monetary, fiscal, or other forces on aggregate nominal demand may depend on how employment and price levels react. A full analysis will clearly have to treat the two issues jointly. Yet there is a considerable measure of independence between them. To a first approximation, the effects on employment and price levels may depend only on the magnitude of the change in aggregate nominal demand, not on its source. On both issues, professional opinion today is very different than it was just after World War II because experience contradicted tentatively accepted hypotheses. Either issue could therefore serve to illustrate my main thesis. I have chosen to deal with only one in order to keep this lecture within reasonable bounds. I have chosen to make that one the relation between inflation and unemployment, because recent experience leaves me less satisfied with the adequacy of my earlier work on that issue than with the adequacy of my earlier work on the forces producing changes in aggregate nominal demand.

II
STAGE I: NEGATIVELY SLOPING PHILLIPS CURVE

Professional analysis of the relation between inflation and unemployment has gone through two stages since the end of World War II and is now entering a third. The first stage was the acceptance of a hypothesis associated with the name of A. W. Phillips that there is a stable negative relation between the level of unemployment and the rate of change of wages — high levels of unemployment being accompanied by falling wages, low levels of unemployment by rising wages (24). The wage change in turn was linked to price change by allowing for the secular increase in productivity and treating the excess of price over wage cost as given by a roughly constant mark-up factor.

Figure I illustrates this hypothesis, where I have followed the standard practice of relating unemployment directly to price change, short-circuiting the intermediate step through wages.

This relation was widely interpreted as a casual relation that offered a stable trade-off to policy-makers. They could choose a low unemployment target, such as U_L. In that case they would have to accept an inflation rate of A. There would remain the problem of choosing the measures (monetary, fiscal, perhaps other) that would produce the level of aggregate nominal demand required to achieve U_L, but if that were done, there need be no concern about maintaining that combination of unemployment and inflation. Alternatively, the policy-makers could choose a low inflation rate or even deflation as their target. In that case they would have to reconcile themselves to higher unemployment: U_O for zero inflation, U_H for deflation.

Economists then busied themselves with trying to extract the relation depicted in Figure I from evidence for different countries and periods, to eliminate the effect of extraneous disturbances, to clarify the relation between wage change and price change, and so on. In addition, they explored social gains and losses from inflation on the one hand and unemployment on the other, in order to facilitate the choice of the 'right' trade-off.

Unfortunately for this hypothesis, additional evidence failed to conform to it. Empirical estimates of the Phillips curve relation were unsatisfactory. More important, the inflation rate that appeared to be consistent with a specified level of unemployment did not remain fixed: in the circumstances of the post-World War II period, when governments everywhere were seeking to promote 'full employment', it tended in any one country to rise over time and to vary sharply among countries. Looked at the other way, rates of inflation that had earlier been associated with low levels of unemployment were experienced along with high levels of unemployment. The phenomenon of simultaneous high inflation and high unemployment increasingly forced itself on public and professional notice, receiving the unlovely label of 'stagflation'.

Some of us were sceptical from the outset about the validity

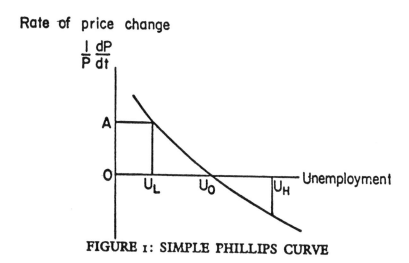

FIGURE 1: SIMPLE PHILLIPS CURVE

of a stable Phillips curve, primarily on theoretical rather than empirical grounds [(2),(3),(4)]. What mattered for employment, we argued, was not wages in dollars or pounds or kronor but real wages — what the wages would buy in goods and services. Low unemployment would, indeed, mean pressure for a higher real wage — but real wages could be higher even if nominal wages were lower, provided that prices were still lower. Similarly, high unemployment would, indeed, mean pressure for a lower real wage — but real wages could be lower, even if nominal wages were higher, provided prices were still higher.

There is no need to assume a stable Phillips curve in order to explain the apparent tendency for an acceleration of inflation to reduce unemployment. That can be explained by the impact of *unanticipated* changes in nominal demand on markets characterised by (implicit or explicit) long-term commitments with respect to both capital and labour. Long-term labour commitments can be explained by the cost of acquiring information by employers about employees and by employees about alternative employment opportunities plus the specific human capital that makes an employee's value to a particular employer grow over time and exceed his value to other potential employers.

Only surprises matter. If everyone anticipated that prices would rise at, say, 20 per cent a year, then this anticipation would be embodied in future wage (and other) contracts, real wages would then behave precisely as they would if everyone anticipated no price rise, and there would be no reason for the 20 per cent rate of inflation to be associated with a different level of unemployment than a zero rate. An unanticipated change is very different, especially in the presence of long-term commitments — themselves partly a result of the imperfect knowledge whose effect they enhance and spread over time. Long-term commitments mean, first, that there is not instantaneous market clearing (as in markets for perishable foods) but only a lagged adjustment of both prices and quantity to changes in demand or supply (as in the house-rental market); second, that commitments entered into depend not only on current observable prices, but also on the prices expected to prevail throughout the term of the commitment.

III

STAGE 2: THE NATURAL RATE HYPOTHESIS

Proceeding along these lines, we [in particular, E. S. Phelps and myself (4),(22),(23)] developed an alternative hypothesis that distinguished between the short-run and long-run effects of unanticipated changes in aggregate nominal demand. Start from some initial stable position and let there be, for example, an unanticipated acceleration of aggregate nominal demand. This will come to each producer as an unexpectedly favourable demand for his product. In an environment in which changes are always occurring in the relative demand for different goods, he will not know whether this change is special to him or pervasive. It will be rational for him to interpret it as at least partly special and to react to it, by seeking to produce more to sell at what he now perceives to be a higher than expected market price for future output. He will be willing to pay higher nominal wages than he had been willing to pay before in order to attract additional workers. The real wage that matters to him is the wage in terms of the price of his product, and he perceives that price as higher than before.

A higher nominal wage can therefore mean a lower *real* wage as perceived by him.

To workers, the situation is different: what matters to them is the purchasing power of wages not over the particular good they produce but over all goods in general. Both they and their employers are likely to adjust more slowly their perception of prices in general — because it is more costly to acquire information about that — than their perception of the price of the particular good they produce. As a result, a rise in nominal wages may be perceived by workers as a rise in real wages and hence call forth an increased supply, at the same time that it is perceived by employers as a fall in real wages and hence calls forth an increased offer of jobs. Expressed in terms of the average of perceived future prices, real wages are lower; in terms of the perceived future average price, real wages are higher.

But this situation is temporary: let the higher rate of growth of aggregate nominal demand and of prices continue, and perceptions will adjust to reality. When they do, the initial effect will disappear, and then even be reversed for a time as workers and employers find themselves locked into inappropriate contracts. Ultimately, employment will be back at the level that prevailed before the assumed unanticipated acceleration in aggregate nominal demand.

This alternative hypothesis is depicted in Figure 2 (p. 90). Each negatively sloping curve is a Phillips curve like that in Figure I except that it is for a particular anticipated or perceived rate of inflation, defined as the perceived average rate of price change, *not* the average of perceived rates of individual price change (the order of the curves would be reversed for the second concept). Start from point E and let the rate of inflation for whatever reason move from A to B and stay there. Unemployment would initially decline to U_L at point F, moving along the curve defined for an anticipated rate of inflation $\left(\frac{1}{P}\frac{dP}{dt}\right)^*$ of A. As anticipations adjusted, the short-run curve would move upward, ultimately to the curve defined for an anticipated inflation rate of B. Concurrently unemployment would move gradually over from F to G. [For a fuller discussion, see (5).]

This analysis is, of course, over-simplified. It supposes a single unanticipated change, whereas, of course, there is a continuing stream of unanticipated changes; it does not deal explicitly with lags, or with overshooting; or with the process of formation of anticipations. But it does highlight the key points: what matters is not inflation *per se,* but unanticipated inflation; there is no stable

Rate of inflation

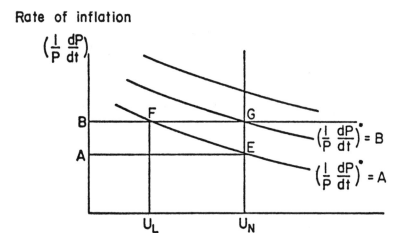

$$\left(\frac{1}{P}\frac{dP}{dt}\right)$$

FIGURE 2: EXPECTATIONS – ADJUSTED PHILLIPS CURVE

trade-off between inflation and unemployment; there is a 'natural rate of unemployment' (U_N), which is consistent with the real forces and with accurate perceptions; unemployment can be kept below that level only by an accelerating inflation; or above it, only by accelerating deflation.

The 'natural rate of unemployment', a term I introduced to parallel Knut Wicksell's 'natural rate of interest', is not a numerical constant but depends on 'real' as opposed to monetary factors — the effectiveness of the labour market, the extent of competition or monopoly, the barriers or encouragements to working in various occupations, and so on.

For example, the natural rate has clearly been rising in the United States for two major reasons. First, women, teenagers, and part-time workers have been constituting a growing fraction of the labour force. These groups are more mobile in employment than other workers, entering and leaving the labour market, shifting more frequently between jobs. As a result, they tend to experience higher average rates of unemployment. Second, unemployment insurance and other forms of assistance to unemployed persons have been made available to more categories of workers, and have become more generous in duration and amount. Workers who lose their jobs are under less pressure to look for other work, will tend to wait longer in the hope, generally fulfilled, of being recalled to their former employment, and can be more selective in the alternatives they consider. Further, the availability of unemployment insurance makes it more attractive to enter the labour force in the first place, and so may itself have stimulated the growth that has occurred in the labour force as a percentage of the population and also its changing composition.

The determinants of the natural rate of unemployment deserve much fuller analysis for both the United States and other countries. So also do the meaning of the recorded unemployment figures and the relation between the recorded figures and the natural rate. These issues are all of the utmost importance for public policy. However, they are side issues for my present limited purpose.

The connection between the state of employment and the level of efficiency or productivity of an economy is another topic that is of fundamental importance for public policy but is a side issue for my present purpose. There is a tendency to take it for granted that a high level of recorded unemployment is evidence of inefficient use of resources and conversely. This view is seriously in error. A low level of unemployment may be a sign of forced-draft economy that is using its resources inefficiently and is inducing workers to sacrifice leisure for goods that they value less highly than the leisure under the mistaken belief that their real wages will be higher than they prove to be. Or a low natural rate of unemployment may reflect institutional arrangements that inhibit change. A highly static rigid economy may have a fixed place for everyone whereas a dynamic, highly progressive economy, which offers ever-changing opportunities and fosters flexibility, may have a high natural rate of unemployment. To illustrate how the same rate may correspond to very different conditions: both Japan and the United Kingdom had low average rates of unemployment from, say, 1950 to 1970, but Japan experienced rapid growth, the UK, stagnation.

The 'natural-rate' or 'accelerationist' or 'expectations-adjusted Phillips curve' hypothesis — as it has been variously designated — is by now widely accepted by economists, though by no means universally. A few still cling to the original Phillips curve; more recognise the difference between short-run and long-run curves but regard even the long-run curve as negatively sloped, though more steeply so than the short-run curves; some substitute a stable relation between the acceleration of inflation and unemployment for a stable relation between inflation and unemployment — aware of, but not concerned about, the possibility that the same logic that drove them to a second derivative will drive them to ever higher derivatives.

Much current economic research is devoted to exploring various aspects of this second stage — the dynamics of the process, the formation of expectations, and the kind of systematic policy, if any, that can have a predictable effect on real magnitudes. We can expect rapid progress on these issues. (Special mention should be made of the work on 'rational expectations', especially the seminal contributions of John Muth, Robert Lucas, and Thomas Sargent.) [Gordon(9).]

IV
STAGE 3: A POSITIVELY SLOPED PHILLIPS CURVE?

Although the second stage is far from having been fully explored, let alone fully absorbed into the economic literature, the course of events is already producing a move to a third stage. In recent years, higher inflation has often been accompanied by higher not lower unemployment, especially for periods of several years in length. A simple statistical Phillips curve for such periods seems to be positively sloped, not vertical. The third stage is directed at accommodating this apparent empirical phenomenon. To do so, I suspect that it will have to include in the analysis the interdependence of economic experience and political developments. It will have to treat at least some political phenomena not as independent variables — as exogenous variables in econometric jargon — but as themselves determined by economic events — as endogenous variables [Gordon (8)]. The second stage was greatly influenced by two major developments in economic theory of the past few decades — one, the analysis of imperfect information and of the cost of acquiring information, pioneered by George Stigler; the other, the role of human capital in determining the form of labour contracts, pioneered by Gary Becker. The third stage will, I believe, be greatly influenced by a third major development — the application of economic analysis to political behaviour, a field in which pioneering work has also been done by Stigler and Becker as well as by Kenneth Arrow, Duncan Black, Anthony Downs, James Buchanan, Gordon Tullock, and others.

The apparent positive relation between inflation and unemployment has been a source of great concern to government policymakers. Let me quote from a recent speech by Prime Minister Callaghan of Great Britain:

'We used to think that you could spend your way out of a recession, and increase employment by cutting taxes and boosting Government spending. I tell you, in all candour, that that option no longer exists, and that, insofar as it ever did exist, it only worked by . . . injecting bigger doses of inflation into the economy, followed by higher levels of unemployment as the next step. . . . That is the history of the past 20 years'. (Speech to Labour Party Conference, 28 September 1976.)

The same view is expressed in a Canadian Government white paper:

'Continuing inflation, particularly in North America, has been accompanied by an increase in measured unemployment rates.' ('The Way Ahead: A Framework for Discussion', Government of Canada Working Paper, October 1976.)

These are remarkable statements, running as they do directly counter to the policies adopted by almost every Western government throughout the post-war period.

(a) Some evidence

More systematic evidence for the past two decades is given

in Table I and Figures 3 and 4, which show the rates of inflation and unemployment in seven industrialised countries over the past two decades. According to the five-year averages in Table I, the rate of inflation and the level of unemployment moved in opposite directions — the expected simple Phillips curve outcome — in five out of seven countries between the first two quinquennia (1956-60, 1961-65); in only four out of seven countries between the second and third quinquennia (1961-65 and 1966-70); and in only one

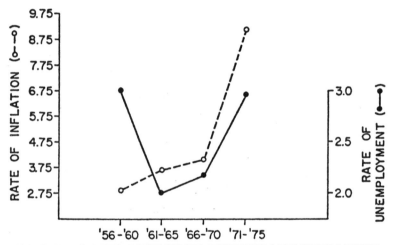

FIGURE 3: RATES OF UNEMPLOYMENT AND INFLATION, 1956 TO 1975, BY QUINQUENNIA: UNWEIGHTED AVERAGE FOR SEVEN COUNTRIES.

of seven countries between the final two quinquennia (1966-70 and 1970-75). And even the one exception — Italy — is not a real exception. True, unemployment averaged a shade lower from 1971 to 1975 than in the prior five years, despite a more than tripling of the rate of inflation. However, since 1973, both inflation and unemployment have risen sharply.

TABLE I

Inflation and unemployment in seven countries, 1956 to 1975: Average values for successive quinquennia

DP = Rate of price change, per cent per year

U = Unemployment, percentage of labour force

	France		Germany		Italy		Japan		Sweden		United Kingdom		United States		Unweighted Average	
	DP	U	DP	U	DP	U	DP	U	DP	U	DP	U	DP	U	DP	U
1956 through 1960	5.6	1.1	1.8	2.9	1.9	6.7	1.9	1.4	3.7	1.9	2.6	1.5	2.0	5.2	2.8	3.0
1961 through 1965	3.7	1.2	2.8	0.7	4.9	3.1	6.2	0.9	3.6	1.2	3.5	1.6	1.3	5.5	3.7	2.0
1966 through 1970	4.4	1.7	2.4	1.2	3.0	3.5	5.4	1.1	4.6	1.6	4.6	2.1	4.2	3.9	4.1	2.2
1971 through 1975	8.8	2.5	6.1	2.1	11.3	3.3	11.4	1.4	7.9	1.8	13.0	3.2	6.7	6.1	9.3	2.9

Note: DP is rate of change of consumer prices compounded annually from calendar year 1955 to 1960; 1960 to 1965; 1965 to 1970; 1970 to 1975. U is average unemployment during five indicated calendar years. As a result, DP is dated one-half year prior to associated U.

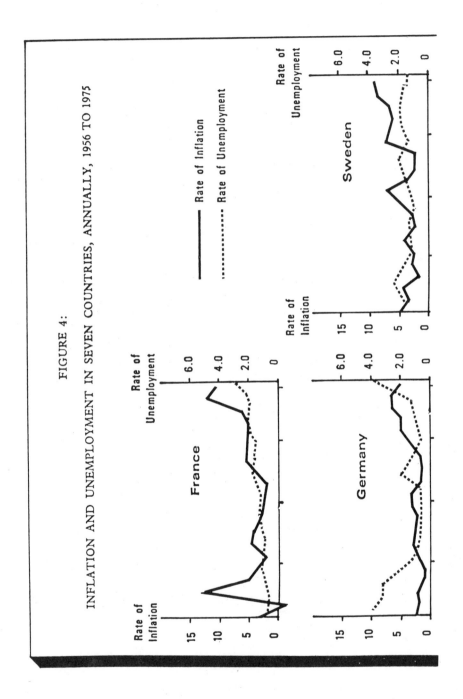

FIGURE 4:

INFLATION AND UNEMPLOYMENT IN SEVEN COUNTRIES, ANNUALLY, 1956 TO 1975

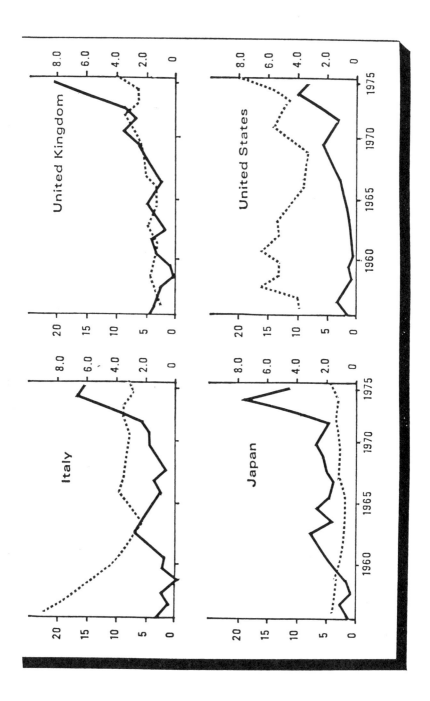

The averages for all seven countries plotted in Figure 3 bring out even more clearly the shift from a negatively sloped simple Phillips curve to a positively sloped one. The two curves move in opposite directions between the first two quinquennia; in the same direction thereafter.

The annual data in Figure 4 tell a similar, though more confused, story. In the early years, there is wide variation in the relation between prices and unemployment, varying from essentially no relation, as in Italy, to a fairly clear-cut year-to-year negative relation, as in the UK and the US. In recent years, however, France, the US, the UK, Germany and Japan all show a clearly marked rise in both inflation and unemployment — though for Japan, the rise in unemployment is much smaller relative to the rise in inflation than in the other countries, reflecting the different meaning of unemployment in the different institutional environment of Japan. Only Sweden and Italy fail to conform to the general pattern.

Of course, these data are at most suggestive. We do not really have seven independent bodies of data. Common international influences affect all countries so that multiplying the number of countries does not multiply proportionately the amount of evidence. In particular, the oil crisis hit all seven countries at the same time. Whatever effect the crisis had on the rate of inflation, it directly disrupted the productive process and tended to increase unemployment. Any such increases can hardly be attributed to the acceleration of inflation that accompanied them; at most the two could be regarded as at least partly the common result of a third influence [Gordon (7)].

Both the quenquennial and annual data show that the oil crisis cannot wholly explain the phenomenon described so graphically by Mr. Callaghan. Already before the quadrupling of oil prices in 1973, most countries show a clearly marked association of rising inflation and rising unemployment. But this too may reflect independent forces rather than the influence of inflation on unemployment. For example, the same forces that have been raising the natural rate of unemployment in the US may have been operating in other countries and may account for their rising trend of unemployment, independently of the consequences of inflation.

Despite these qualifications, the data strongly suggest that, at least in some countries, of which Britain, Canada, and Italy may be the best examples, rising inflation and rising unemployment have been mutually reinforcing, rather than the separate effects of separate causes. The data are not inconsistent with the stronger statement that, in all industrialised countries, higher rates of inflation have some effects that, at least for a time, make for higher unemployment. The rest of this paper is devoted to a preliminary exploration of what some of these effects may be.

(b) A tentative hypothesis

I conjecture that a modest elaboration of the natural-rate hypothesis is all that is required to account for a positive relation between inflation and unemployment, though of course such a positive relation may also occur for other reasons. Just as the natural-rate hypothesis explains a negatively sloped Phillips curve over short periods as a temporary phenomenon that will disappear as economic agents adjust their expectations to reality, so a positively sloped Phillips curve over somewhat longer periods may occur as a transitional phenomenon that will disappear as economic agents adjust not only their expectations but their institutional and political arrangements to a new reality. When this is achieved, I believe that — as the natural-rate hypothesis suggests — the rate of unemployment will be largely independent of the average rate of inflation, though the efficiency of utilisation of resources may not be. High inflation need not mean either abnormally high or abnormally low unemployment. However, the institutional and political arrangements that accompany it, either as relics of earlier history or as products of the inflation itself, are likely to prove antithetical to the most productive use of employed resources — a special case of the distinction between the state of employment and the productivity of an economy referred to earlier.

Experience in many Latin American countries that have adjusted to chronically high inflation rates — experience that has been analysed most perceptively by some of my colleagues, particularly Arnold Harberger and Larry Sjaastad [(12),(25)] — is consistent, I believe, with this view.

In the version of the natural-rate hypothesis summarised in

Figure 2, the vertical curve is for alternative rates of fully anticipated inflation. Whatever that rate — be it negative, zero or
positive — it can be built into every decision if it is fully anticipated. At an anticipated 20 per cent per year inflation, for example, long-term wage contracts would provide for a wage in each
year that would rise relative to the zero-inflation wage by just 20
per cent per year; long-term loans would bear an interest rate 20
percentage points higher than the zero-inflation rate, or a principal
that would be raised by 20 per cent a year; and so on — in short,
the equivalent of a full indexing of all contracts. The high rate
of inflation would have some real effects, by altering desired cash
balances, for example, but it need not alter the efficiency of labour
markets, or the length or terms of labour contracts, and hence,
it need not change the natural rate of unemployment.

This analysis implicitly supposes, first, that inflation is steady
or at least no more variable ·at a high rate than at a low —
otherwise, it is unlikely that inflation would be as fully anticipated
at high as at low rates of inflation; second, that the inflation is,
or can be, open, with all prices free to adjust to the higher rate,
so that relative price adjustments are the same with a 20 per cent
inflation as with a zero inflation; third, really a variant of the second point, that there are no obstacles to indexing of contracts.

Ultimately, if inflation at an average rate of 20 per cent per
year were to prevail for many decades, these requirements could
come fairly close to being met, which is why I am inclined to retain
the long-long-run vertical Phillips curve. But when a country initially moves to higher rates of inflation, these requirements will
be systematically departed from. And such a transitional period
may well extend over decades.

Consider, in particular, the US and the UK. For two centuries before World War II for the UK, and a century and a half
for the US, prices varied about a roughly constant level, showing
substantial increases in time of war, then post-war declines to
roughly pre-war levels. The concept of a 'normal' price level was
deeply embedded in the financial and other institutions of the two
countries and in the habits and attitudes of their citizens.

In the immediate post-World War II period, prior experience
was widely expected to recur. The fact was post-war inflation

superimposed on wartime inflation; yet the expectation in both the US and the UK was deflation. It took a long time for the fear of post-war deflation to dissipate — if it still has — and still longer before expectations started to adjust to the fundamental change in the monetary system. That adjustment is still far from complete [Klein (16)].

Indeed, we do not know what a complete adjustment will consist of. We cannot know now whether the industrialised countries will return to the pre-World War II pattern of a long-term stable price level, or will move toward the Latin American pattern of chronically high inflation rates — with every now and then an acute outbreak of super- or hyper-inflation, as occurred recently in Chile and Argentina [Harberger (11)] — or will undergo more radical economic and political change leading to a still different resolution of the present ambiguous situation.

This uncertainty — or more precisely, the circumstances producing this uncertainty — leads to systematic departures from the conditions required for a vertical Phillips curve.

The most fundamental departure is that a high inflation rate is not likely to be steady during the transition decades. Rather, the higher the rate, the more variable it is likely to be. That has been empirically true of differences among countries in the past several decades [Jaffe and Kleiman (14); Logue and Willett (17)]. It is also highly plausible on theoretical grounds — both about actual inflation and, even more clearly, the anticipations of economic agents with respect to inflation. Governments have not produced high inflation as a deliberate announced policy but as a consequence of other policies — in particular, policies of full employment and welfare state policies raising government spending. They all proclaim their adherence to the goal of stable prices. They do so in response to their constituents, who may welcome many of the side-effects of inflation, but are still wedded to the concept of stable money. A burst of inflation produces strong pressure to counter it. Policy goes from one direction to the other, encouraging wide variation in the actual and anticipated rate of inflation. And, of course, in such an environment, no one has single-valued anticipations. Everyone recognises that there is great uncertainty about what actual inflation will turn out to be over any specific future interval [Jaffe and Kleiman (14); Meiselman (20)].

The tendency for inflation that is high on the average to be highly variable is reinforced by the effect of inflation on the political cohesiveness of a country in which institutional arrangements and financial contracts have been adjusted to a long-term 'normal' price level. Some groups gain (e.g., home owners); others lose (e.g., owners of savings accounts and fixed interest securities). 'Prudent' behaviour becomes in fact reckless, and 'reckless' behaviour in fact prudent. The society is polarised; one group is set against another. Political unrest increases. The capacity of any government to govern is reduced at the same time that the pressure for strong action grows.

An increased variability of actual or anticipated inflation may raise the natural rate of unemployment in two rather different ways.

First, increased volatility shortens the optimum length of unindexed commitments and renders indexing more advantageous [Gray (10)]. But it takes time for actual practice to adjust. In the meantime, prior arrangements introduce rigidities that reduce the effectiveness of markets. An additional element of uncertainty is, as it were, added to every market arrangement. In addition, indexing is, even at best, an imperfect substitute for stability of the inflation rate. Price indexes are imperfect; they are available only with a lag, and generally are applied to contract terms only with a further lag.

These developments clearly lower economic efficiency. It is less clear what their effect is on recorded unemployment. High average inventories of all kinds is one way to meet increased rigidity and uncertainty. But that may mean labour-hoarding by enterprises and low unemployment or a larger force of workers between jobs and so high unemployment. Shorter commitments may mean more rapid adjustment of employment to changed conditions and so low unemployment, or the delay in adjusting the length of commitments may lead to less satisfactory adjustment and so high unemployment. Clearly, much additional research is necessary in this area to clarify the relative importance of the various effects. About all one can say now is that the slow adjustment of commitments and the imperfections of indexing may contribute to the recorded increase in unemployment.

A second related effect of increased volatility of inflation is to render market prices a less efficient system for co-ordinating economic activity. A fundamental function of a price system, as Hayek (13) emphasised so brilliantly, is to transmit compactly, efficiently, and at low cost the information that economic agents need in order to decide what to produce and how to produce it, or how to employ owned resources. The relevant information is about *relative* prices — of one product relative to another, of the services of one factor of production relative to another, of products relative to factor services, of prices now relative to prices in the future. But the information in practice is transmitted in the form of *absolute* prices — prices in dollars or pounds or kronor. If the price level is on the average stable or changing at a steady rate, it is relatively easy to extract the signal about relative prices from the observed absolute prices. The more volatile the rate of general inflation, the harder it becomes to extract the signal about relative prices from the absolute prices: the broadcast about relative prices is as it were being jammed by the noise coming from the inflation broadcast [Lucas (18), (19); Harberger (11)]. At the extreme, the system of absolute prices becomes nearly useless, and economic agents resort either to an alternative currency, or to barter, with disastrous effects on productivity.

Again, the effect on economic efficiency is clear, on unemployment less so. But, again, it seems plausible that the average level of unemployment would be raised by the increased amount of noise in market signals, at least during the period when institutional arrangements are not yet adapted to the new situation.

These effects of increased volatility of inflation would occur even if prices were legally free to adjust — if, in that sense, the inflation were open. In practice, the distorting effects of uncertainty, rigidity of voluntary long-term contracts, and the contamination of price signals will almost certainly be reinforced by legal restrictions on price change. In the modern world, governments are themselves producers of services sold on the market: from postal services to a wide range of other items. Other prices are regulated by government, and require government approval for change: from air fares to taxicab fares to charges for electricity. In these cases, governments cannot avoid being involved in the price-fixing process. In addition, the social and political forces unleashed by volatile inflation rates will lead governments to try to repress inflation in still other areas: by explicit price and wage control, or by pressuring private business or unions 'voluntarily' to exercise 'restraint', or by speculating in foreign exchange in order to alter the exchange rate.

The details will vary from time to time and from country to country, but the general result is the same: reduction in the capacity of the price system to guide economic activity; distortions in relative prices because of the introduction of greater friction, as it were, in all markets; and, very likely, a higher recorded rate of unemployment [(5)].

The forces I have just described may render the political and economic system dynamically unstable and produce hyper-inflation and radical political change — as in many defeated countries after World War I, or in Chile and Argentina more recently. At the other extreme, before any such catastrophe occurs, policies may be adopted that will achieve a relatively low and stable rate of inflation and lead to the dismantling of many of the interferences with the price system. That would re-establish the preconditions for the straightforward natural-rate hypothesis and enable that hypothesis to be used to predict the course of the transition.

An intermediate possibility is that the system will reach stability at a fairly constant though high average rate of inflation. In that case, unemployment should also settle down to a fairly constant level decidedly lower than during the transition. As the preceding discussion emphasises, *increasing* volatility and *increasing* government intervention with the price system are the major factors that seem likely to raise unemployment, not *high* voltility or a *high* level of intervention.

Ways of coping with both volatility and intervention will develop: through indexing and similar arrangements for coping with volatility of inflation; through the development of indirect ways of altering prices and wages for avoiding government controls.

Under these circumstances, the long-run Phillips curve would again be vertical, and we would be back at the natural-rate hypothesis, though perhaps for a different range of inflation rates than that for which it was first suggested.

Because the phenomenon to be explained is the co-existence of high inflation and high unemployment, I have stressed the effect of institutional changes produced by a transition from a monetary system in which there was a 'normal' price level to a monetary system consistent with long periods of high, and possibly highly variable, inflation. It should be noted that once these institutional changes were made, and economic agents had adjusted their practices and anticipations to them, a reversal to the earlier monetary framework or even the adoption in the new monetary framework of a successful policy of low inflation would in its turn require new adjustments, and these might have many of the same adverse transitional effects on the level of employment. There would appear to be an intermediate-run negatively sloped Phillips curve instead of the positively sloped one I have tried to rationalise.

V

CONCLUSION

One consequence of the Keynesian revolution of the 1930s was the acceptance of a rigid absolute wage level, and a nearly rigid absolute price level, as a starting point for analysing short-term economic change. It came to be taken for granted that these were essentially intitutional data and were so regarded by economic agents, so that changes in aggregate nominal demand would be reflected almost entirely in output and hardly at all in prices. The age-old confusion between absolute prices and relative prices gained a new lease on life.

In this intellectual atmosphere it was understandable that economists would analyse the relation between unemployment and *nominal* rather than *real* wages and would implicitly regard changes in anticipated *nominal* wages as equal to changes in anticipated *real* wages. Moreover, the empirical evidence that initially suggested a stable relation between the level of unemployment and the rate of change of nominal wages was drawn from a period when, despite sharp short-period fluctuations in prices, there was a relatively stable long-run price level and when the expectation of continued stability was widely shared. Hence these data flashed no warning signals about the special character of the assumptions.

The hypothesis that there is a stable relation between the level of unemployment and the rate of inflation was adopted by the economics profession with alacrity. It filled a gap in Keynes's theoretical structure. It seemed to be the 'one equation' that Keynes himself had said 'we are . . . short' (15). In addition, it seemed to provide a reliable tool for economic policy, enabling the economist to inform the policy-maker about the alternatives available to him.

As in any science, so long as experience seemed to be consistent with the reigning hypothesis, it continued to be accepted, although, as always, a few dissenters questioned its validity.

But as the 1950s turned into the 1960s, and the 1960s into the 1970s, it became increasingly difficult to accept the hypothesis in its simple form. It seemed to take larger and larger doses of inflation to keep down the level of unemployment. Stagflation reared its ugly head.

Many attempts were made to patch up the hypothesis by allowing for special factors such as the strength of trade unions. But experience stubbornly refused to conform to the patched-up version.

A more radical revision was required. It took the form of stressing the importance of surprises — of differences between actual and anticipated magnitudes. It restored the primacy of the distinction between 'real' and 'nominal' magnitudes. There is a 'natural rate of unemployment' at any time determined by real factors. This natural rate will tend to be attained when expectations are on the average realised. The same real situation is consistent with any absolute level of prices or of price change, provided allowance is made for the effect of price change on the real cost of holding money balances. In this respect, money is neutral. On the other hand, unanticipated changes in aggregate nominal demand and in inflation will cause systematic errors of perception on the part of employers and employees alike that will initially lead unemployment to deviate in the opposite direction from its natural rate. In this respect, money is not neutral. However, such deviations are transitory, though it may take a long chronological time before they are reversed and finally eliminated as anticipations adjust.

The natural-rate hypothesis contains the original Phillips curve hypothesis as a special case and rationalises a far broader range of experience, in particular the phenomenon of stagflation. It has by now been widely though not universally accepted.

However, the natural-rate hypothesis in its present form has not proved rich enough to explain a more recent development — a move from stagflation to slumpflation. In recent years, higher inflation has often been accompanied by higher unemployment — not lower unemployment, as the single Phillips curve would suggest, nor the same unemployment, as the natural-rate hypothesis would suggest.

This recent association of higher inflation with higher unemployment may reflect the common impact of such events as the oil crisis, or independent forces that have imparted a common upward trend to inflation and unemployment.

However, a major factor in some countries and a contributing factor in others may be that they are in a transitional period — this time to be measured by quinquennia or decades, not years. The public has not adapted its attitudes or its institutions to a new monetary environment. Inflation tends not only to be higher but also increasingly volatile and to be accompanied by widening government intervention into the setting of prices. The growing volatility of inflation and the growing departure of relative prices from the values that market forces alone would set combine to render the economic system less efficient, to introduce frictions in all markets, and, very likely, to raise the recorded rate of unemployment.

On this analysis, the present situation cannot last. it will either degenerate into hyper-inflation and radical change; or institutions will adjust to a situation of chronic inflation; or governments will adopt policies that will produce a low rate of inflation and less government intervention into the fixing of prices.

I have told a perfectly standard story of how scientific theories are revised. Yet it is a story that has far-reaching importance.

Government policy about inflation and unemployment has

been at the centre of political controversy. Ideological war has raged over these matters. Yet the drastic change that has occurred in economic theory has not been a result of ideological warfare. It has not resulted from divergent political beliefs or aims. It has responded almost entirely to the force of events: brute experience proved far more potent than the strongest of political or ideological preferences.

The importance for humanity of a correct understanding of positive economic science is vividly brought out by a statement made nearly two hundred years ago by Pierre S. du Pont, a Deputy from Nemours to the French National Assembly, speaking, appropriately enough, on a proposal to issue additional *assignats* — the fiat money of the French Revolution:

'Gentlemen, it is a disagreeable custom to which one is too easily led by the harshness of the discussions, to assume evil intentions. It is necessary to be gracious as to intentions; one should believe them good, and apparently they are; but we do not have to be gracious at all to inconsistent logic or to absurd reasoning. Bad logicians have committed more involuntary crimes than bad men have done intentionally.' (25 September 1790.)

References

(1) Milton Friedman, 'The Methodology of Positive Economics', *Essays in Positive Economics* (Chicago: University of Chicago Press, 1953).

(2) —, 'What Price Guideposts?', in G. P. Shultz and R. Z. Aliber (eds.), *Guidelines: Informal Contracts and the Market Place* (Chicago: University of Chicago Press, 1966), pp. 17-39 and 55-61.

(3) —, 'An Inflationary Recession', *Newsweek*, 17 October, 1966.

(4) —, 'The Role of Monetary Policy', *American Economic Review*, 58 (March 1968), pp. 1-17.

(5) —, *Price Theory* (Chicago: Aldine Publishing Co., 1976), ch. 12.

(6) —, *Inflation: Causes and Consequences* (Bombay: Asia Publishing House, 1963), reprinted in *Dollars and Deficits* (Englewood Cliffs, N.J.: Prentice-Hall, 1968), pp. 21-71.

(7) Robert J. Gordon, 'Alternative Responses of Policy to External Supply Shocks', *Brookings Papers on Economic Activity*, No. 1 (1975), pp. 183-206.

(8) —, 'The Demand and Supply of Inflation', *Journal of Law and Economics*, 18 (December 1975), pp. 807-836.

(9) —, 'Recent Developments in the Theory of Inflation and Unemployment', *Journal of Monetary Economics*, 2 (1976), pp. 185-219.

(10) Jo Anna Gray, 'Essays on Wage Indexation', unpublished Ph.D. dissertation, University of Chicago, 1976.

(11) Arnold C. Harberger, 'Inflation', *The Great Ideas Today, 1976* (Chicago: Encyclopaedia Britannica, Inc., 1976), pp. 95-106.

(12) —, 'The Inflation Problem in Latin America', a report prepared for the Buenos Aires (March 1966) meeting of the Inter-American Committee of the Alliance for Progress, published in Spanish as 'El problema de la inflación en América Latina', in Centro de Estudios Monetarios Latinoamericanos, *Boletín Mensual,* June 1966, pp. 253-269; reprinted in Economic Development Institute, *Trabajos sobre desarrollo económico* (Washington, D.C.: IBRD, 1967).

(13) F. A. Hayek, 'The Use of Knowledge in Society', *American*

999999999

Economic Review, 35 (September 1945), pp. 519-530.

(14) Dwight Jaffe and Ephraim Kleiman, 'The Welfare Implications of Uneven Inflation', Seminar paper No. 50, Institute for International Economic Studies, University of Stockholm, November 1975.

(15) J. M. Keynes, *General Theory of Employment, Interest, and Money* (London: Macmillan, 1936), p. 276.

(16) Benjamin Klein, 'Our New Monetary Standard: The Measurement and Effects of Price Uncertainty, 1880-1973', *Economic Inquiry,* December 1975, pp. 461-483.

(17) Dennis E. Logue and Thomas D. Willett, 'A Note on the Relation between the Rate and Variability of Inflation', *Economica,* May 1976, pp. 151-158.

(18) Robert E. Lucas, 'Some International Evidence on Output-Inflation Tradeoffs', *American Economic Review,* 63 (June 1973), pp. 326-334.

(19) —, 'An Equilibrium Model of the Business Cycle', *Journal of Political Economy,* 83 (December 1975), pp. 1,113-1,144.

(20) David Meiselman, 'Capital Formation, Monetary and Financial Adjustments', *Proceedings,* 27th National Conference of Tax Foundation, 1976, pp. 9-15.

(21) John Muth, 'Rational Expectations and the Theory of Price Movements', *Econometrica,* 29 (July 1961), pp. 315-333.

(22) E. S. Phelps, 'Phillips Curve, Expectations of Inflation and Optimal Unemployment Over Time', *Economica,* 34 (August 1967), pp. 254-281.

(23) —, 'Money Wage Dynamics and Labour Market Equilibrium', in E. S. Phelps (ed.), *Microeconomic Foundations of Employment and Inflation Theory* (New York: Norton, 1970).

(24) A. W. Phillips 'The Relationship between Unemployment and the Rate of Change of Money Wage Rates in the United Kingdom, 1861-1957', *Economica,* November 1958, pp. 283-299.

(25) Larry A. Sjaastad, 'Monetary Policy and Suppressed Inflation in Latin America', in R. Z. Aliber (ed.), *National Monetary Policies and the International Financial System* (Chicago: University of Chicago Press, 1974), pp. 127-138.